Savage Bitches

Elsa Coulter

Published by Trellis Publishing, 2021.

SAVAGE BITCHES

First edition. July 3, 2021.

Copyright © 2021 Elsa Coulter.

ISBN: 979-8224720026

Written by Elsa Coulter.

SAVAGE BITCHES

ELSA COULTER

IRENE MASLIN

Despite being a bit rough around the edges, many of the townspeople residing in the rural countryside of Mirboo North in Victoria, Australia would vouch for 28-year-old motorcycle enthusiast Paul Snabel. It was true that the young man had a penchant for reckless driving. heavy drinking, and frequent drug use; however, those that knew him best saw straight through his bad boy facade. He was often described as openly affectionate and he cared deeply for his family. People enjoyed being around Paul, despite his flaws. In fact, Paul's magnetic personality made him the sort of man with plenty of friends and very few enemies.

When Paul disappeared suddenly after attending a party at the home of Donna Randall in November 1989, his flatmate was not immediately concerned for his well being. After binging on a cocktail of drugs and alcohol, Snabel would sometimes be prone to taking off on impromptu joyrides across the open roads. Even after a week or so without any contact, loved ones did not suspect that Paul could have possibly been the victim of a violent crime. Instead, people assumed that he had finally succumbed to his vices. Suspecting that he may have careened off of a steep cliff in a drunken stupor, local authorities proceeded to conduct an extensive search along Victoria's highways.

Instead of recovering a body, police were surprised to find pieces of Snabel's most prized possession – a red and white striped Yamaha motorcycle – disassembled across several garbage dumps and dams. In the coming weeks, the abandoned pieces would prove to be the first of many clues pointing to a stunning conspiracy revolved around love lost and a callous, brutal murder, unlike anything the area had experienced before or since.

* * *

Police first began to seriously suspect foul play upon receiving a report from a farmer who had stumbled upon a lone bike engine.

Though authorities were sure that the engine was in fact consistent with the model whose scattered parts were surfacing across the countryside, it became evident upon closer investigation that someone had attempted to file off the vehicle's serial number. Puzzled, investigators had little choice but to retrace Paul's steps – which quickly led them to Donna Randall and her sister, Karen.

The Randall sisters were no strangers to Snabel; in fact, it quickly became apparent that Karen and Paul had been involved in a volatile relationship for a number of years. At the time of his disappearance, the two were separated; Paul's amphetamine use was beginning to spiral out of control, and after a series of physical confrontations, she sought a clean break. However, Snabel was less than thrilled to leave behind Randall. When Karen and her young son moved to a neighboring town in an attempt to escape the toxic environment, Paul tracked down Randall's child and followed him home from school. Upon discovering Karen's new address, he left an intimidating note on the front of her door, causing her a great deal of anxiety and concern.

Nevertheless, the sisters confirmed that Paul had in fact recently attended a house party at Donna's residence despite the troubling history he shared with Karen. Afterward, he had followed the sisters back to mutual friend Rhona Heaney's home. However, the Randall sisters insisted that they had grown tired of his drunken, unruly behavior and had ordered him to leave. Though the authorities were convinced of the women's innocence in the disappearance, they decided to visit Rhona Heaney in hopes of tracking down some significant leads. Once there, Rhona corroborated the story Donna and Karen had provided; the only additional piece of information she was able to provide concerned dropping her children off at the home of Irene Maslin prior to Snabel's arrival.

Feeling that their line of questioning wasn't leading anywhere meaningful, investigators began to instead focus their attention on the recovered bike parts. By the time they had begun questioning suspects, they had recovered enough pieces to almost completely reassemble the bike to its original state. As they began to place the evidence together, they noticed a very peculiar detail; the wiring of the motorcycle had been found neatly coiled and carefully placed in individual plastic bags. As it turned out, those plastic bags were uniquely designed for the state electricity commission. Upon contacting the commission, it was revealed that the bags were not readily available to the general public. After searching through a list of employees and comparing it with the names of individuals involved in the investigation, it was discovered that Irene Maslin's husband, Jano, was an electrician with the state. Having finally found a potential suspect – however tenuous their lead may have been – the police eagerly began to investigate.

* * *

On the surface, Irene Maslin appeared to be nothing more than a typical housewife. After immigrating from Holland as a small child in 1954, she attended high school locally, worked on a farm, and eventually took on a position as a nursing aide in a nearby hospital. After giving birth to a son with a previous husband, Irene met Jano at a Rotary Club meeting and quickly fell in love. Like many of the women in her small town, she enjoyed domestic activities such as cooking and gardening. Although she did not have any children with Jano, she was a well-known maternal figure in the community and frequently served as a "carekeeper". She has a reputation for knitting jumpers and accessories for expectant mothers and newborns. Irene even held an excellent rapport with the local church. With no history of prior arrests, investigators were skeptical that a trip to the Maslin household would yield any answers to the mysterious departure of Paul Snabel.

Playing the part of an average, law-abiding couple, both Jano and Irene were initially cooperative and welcomed the inquisitive investigators to search their home as they pleased. Nothing immediately stood out as suspicious. However, when they reached the garage, they found plastic bags identical to the ones found at the dump as well as several electrical cords neatly coiled in a fashion similar to the wiring recovered from the Yamaha. Lodged in the cracks of the concrete floor, flecks of red paint consistent with that of the motorbike were discovered. Also recovered inside of the garage was a used a metal file, which was covered with remnants of the same red paint.

As evidence began leaving their home for further examination, the Maslin's attitude towards the police quickly became hostile. In contrast to their initial friendliness, Jano Maslin ultimately shooed away the authorities and, on behalf of his wife, insisted that the two had no statement to provide concerning the crime. The next time investigators returned to the Maslin residence, they discovered that the married couple had packed their belongings and left town without any indicator of when they might return. Neighbors asserted that the Maslin's had gone on a Christmas vacation, although it quickly became clear that no one had an idea of where exactly they had traveled to for the holidays.

As the search for the Maslin's began, a very different portrait of Irene was painted by neighbors and friends. The townspeople of Mirboo North, frightened of her "intimidating aura", were hesitant to cross the seemingly harmless woman. The amiable, kind-hearted persona she had presented began to disintegrate as anecdotes recounting her domineering personality and aggressive behavior began to emerge. On one occasion, it was reported that Irene had hired "big blokes" to beat a man that tried her patience. Others confessed that Maslin was a frequent drug trafficker that ran with industry "heavy hitters". According to those individuals, she openly dealt amphetamines and imported kilos of marijuana from New South Wales. Though the line between rumor and reality was hazy at best, one thing became evident; the situation that the police had stumbled into was much more dangerous than they could have initially anticipated.

****

Days passed without a trace of Jano or Irene Maslin. Attention shifted back to Karen Randall, who had checked herself into a local hospital because of her fragile emotional state. When questioned a second time by authorities, she broke down in tears and redacted the original statement she had provided regarding Paul's disappearance. Karen then admitted that Irene had been at Rhona's house on the day of the disappearance, directly contradicting Maslin's previous statements claiming that she had never met Snabel. Several days later, Donna Randall came forward to admit that her prior testimony had been inaccurate as well. Following the hospitalization, Irene and Rhona had begun to suspect that that Karen might be talking to authorities. In an attempt to intimidate the Randall sisters, Heaney and Maslin had fetched Donna in the dead of night and ordered her to keep her sister quiet. Insinuating that their lives may be in danger if they failed to oblige, Donna made the decision to cooperate with police in exchange for safety from her friends turned tormentors.

Just a few days before Paul's disappearance, the Randall sisters had shared afternoon tea with Rhona and Irene. At that time, Karen confided in her friends her concerns regarding the increasingly unstable affair she shared with Snabel. Disgusted by Snabel's behavior, the women began discussing possible solutions to Karen's recurring relationship issues. When someone suggested in jest that they simply kill the man, Irene Maslin in particular latched onto the idea and refused to let go. The master manipulator then goaded the three women into a sinister murder plot.

Following Donna's party, Karen baited the inebriated Snabel into visiting Rhona Heaney's secluded countryside home with promises of rekindling the bond they once shared. Upon his arrival, he was instead greeted by Irene and Rhona, who coerced him into taking some drugs. The women had assured him that the syringes they offered were filled with speed; however, they failed to mention that the amphetamines were laced with corrosive battery acid. Being fully aware that the concentrated sulfuric acid would quickly wreak havoc on Paul's body and result in a gruesome death, Karen and Donna opted to leave Rhona's home once the substance began flowing through his veins. Though neither sister had witnessed the death or viewed the corpse, they hadn't heard from him following the events at the Heaney household. Several days later, Rhona and Irene mentioned having sold the couch Paul sat on because they were unable to remove the stains he left behind. In addition, Irene had organized and constructed the stories each woman provided to officers upon investigation.

Using the information Donna provided, police continued to pursue the Maslin's with new fervor. With a new lead on the location of their vacation getaway, they anxiously arrived at an address in the sparsely populated countryside. Instead of finding their suspects, authorities were greeted by Ian GIllin, an ex-footballer who happened to be friends with the women in question. When asked about his whereabouts during the time of the disappearance, he immediately admitted that he had been with the Maslin's on the day of the crime. He claimed to have spent the day digging the foundation for a new swimming pool in the backyard, and had only briefly met Paul. That evening, Jano Maslin left the property for several hours, then returned with the red and white Yamaha motorcycle. Ian was then ordered to disassemble the bike, and being a simple man, he helped without much question. Jano and Ian then proceeded to scatter the parts of the motorcycle across several dumps, dams, and bushes nearby. Matching the locations of the recovered Yamaha with the locations Ian Gillin referenced in his testimony, it became clear that he was, in fact, the person behind the destruction of Paul Snabel's bike.

With enough damning evidence in their hands to be sure of the women's involvement in Snabel's disappearance, warrants for the arrests of Irene Maslin and Rhona Heaney were filed. When they eventually returned home after their holiday vacation, they were promptly taken into custody.

The two women were reacting to the circumstances in drastically different ways. On one hand, Irene's attitude upon being taken into the station could best be described as contemptuous. As investigators began asking questions concerning the crime, she remained silent and steady. Her stony face showed no signs of guilt or remorse, though it was clear that she had something to hide. Rhona, on the other hand, was anxious and initially hesitant to confirm or deny the truthfulness of her original statements to police. Without letting much time pass, she came to the conclusion that she could not escape punishment. Unwilling to take all of the blame for the heinous crime, she agreed to provide further details regarding the last moments of Paul Snabel's short life.

* * *

Hours after the initial injection of battery acid, it appeared that the poison was not especially effective; rather than collapsing or writhing in pain, Paul continued about his business and even began riding his motorcycle around Heaney's backyard. Frustrated by their failure, the women were forced plan a different course of action. As Snabel remained completely oblivious to the women's evil intentions, Irene made arrangements for Ian Gillin to be dropped off at Rhona's home. There, the two men met for the first time and shared a drink or two. About a half hour into Ian's visit, Maslin pulled the young man aside and informed him that Paul "had to go". She then handed Gillin a child's metal baseball bat and badgered him into hitting Snabel across the head with it. Although the two barely knew each other, Gillin agreed to it out of fear. Immediately, the blow knocked Paul unconscious; during that time, the women forced another dose of battery acid into his body.

Evidently, that wasn't enough to kill him. As Paul began to moan and groan in pain, Irene began to scream at Ian to continue hitting the severely injured man. Startled, Ian Gillin swung the bat several times, fracturing Snabel's skull and splattering blood across the room. Horrified by his own actions, he became sick and stepped away from the battered, dying man. Rhona, equally horrified by the gruesome turn of events, witnessed Irene finish Paul off once and for all. Incredibly, after sustaining a number of hits to the head, he continued to cling to life and gasp for breath. Irene proceeded to grab a plastic bag, place it over the man's bloodied head, and secure it into place with a rubber band. Together, Rhona and Irene watched as their defenseless victim slowly suffocated.

Once the deed was done, Irene's husband and Ian set to work on disposing of the bike. Meanwhile, Irene and Rhona wrapped the body in a plastic tarp and unceremoniously shoved it into the back seat of their Subaru. The two women then drove deep into the isolated bushlands and dumped the corpse far from the nearest town. They also carefully disposed of all of the incriminating evidence involved in the murder.

As the police followed up on Rhona's account, the mystery finally began to gain some clarity. After tracking down Ian GIllin, he confirmed Heaney's version of events. He added crucial details regarding the intimidation tactics Irene employed; when he initially pulled away from the metal baseball bat, Maslin assured him that Paul would kill Karen unless Ian took initiative and killed him first. When Gillin continued to show reservations about murdering Snabel, Maslin began to imply that Ian might find himself in trouble if he did not do as Irene commanded. Asserting that his actions were a measure of self-defense against Irene's wrath, he had no issues taking responsibility for the crime he had committed.

Forensic teams later lifted the lining of Rhona Heaney's living room carpet and found blood stains soaked deep into the base of the floor. Unfortunately, at the time DNA testing was not readily available, making it impossible to know for sure whether or not the blood found beneath the carpet belonged to Paul. Luckily, DNA proof was not necessary for charging the criminals or discovering the fate of Paul Snabel. Using Rhona's account of where the body was dumped, police uncovered scraps of torn clothing and fragments of a human skeleton in the bush. There, they were lucky enough to recover an intact skull and jawbone; Snabel's dental records matched that of the skeleton, finally providing conclusive evidence for family and friends as to where Paul had disappeared to for so many months

* * *

After a bizarre and tumultuous investigation, prosecutors were finally able to take the case to trial and present their evidence to a stunned jury. Although Karen Randall was the impetus behind the murder, she ultimately only received two years in prison for her involvement in the plot to kill her former lover. Her sister, Donna, was awarded an identical sentence. Ian Gillin was charged and found guilty of manslaughter. He served three years behind bars before earning his freedom. The court was much less lenient when it came to jailing Rhona Heaney; she was sentenced to 10 years in prison for the conspiracy. Although her husband Jano was acquitted of any involvement in the crime, Irene eventually confessed to being guilty of murder after spending months in denial. In accordance with Australian law at the time, she received the maximum jail sentence of 15 years.

Irene Maslin has since served her time and has been released from prison. Despite her distinct lack of remorse, nothing could prevent her from being allowed back into the general public. Although her current whereabouts are unknown, her reputation has lived on. The barbarism of her action attracted plenty of media attention, and she has been featured on a number of true crime television shows throughout the years. But perhaps the biggest impact she has made lies deep in the hearts of those that were once close to her. Years after the crime, locals still recall the chills she sent shivering down the spines of her neighbors. Some authorities even likened the magnitude of her evil to infamous serial killer Charles Manson.

With Maslin having assumed a new identity, it's almost impossible to know for certain what drove her lust for blood. Perhaps she was genuinely concerned for the safety of Karen Randall; others hypothesize that Paul Snabel's drug habit may have landed him in debt. Irene may have just been seeking the adrenaline high that comes with taking a life. While her motives cannot be conclusively determined, there is an age old lesson to be learned from the tragedy that unfolded in Mirboo North. Though Irene Maslin appeared to be nothing more than an innocent housewife to some, in reality, she was capable committing savage acts – proving that sometimes, the people we hold in the highest regard turn out to be the people we know the least.

KILLER COUGAR : THE TRUE STORY OF SERIAL KILLER SHEILA LABARRE

DARLA PUGH

PROLOGUE

The farmhouse and surrounding area looked like something from the set of "Little House on the Prairie."

The house on Harvey Farm stood nestled in between tall pine trees, peaceful streams, and wildlife.

A place where you don't expect to find scenes that would be given an "X" rating if it were a horror movie.

The police arrived at the home while conducting a search for a missing young man named Kenneth Countje. They did not have to search far to find evidence of criminal activity. In the front of the property, lay a mattress burning alongside a smoking garbage barrel.

Their first inclination was to believe that the resident was burning garbage. A citation was due, maybe, but they had more pressing matters to attend to.

But upon closer inspection of the barrel, the officers saw a bone sticking out of the garbage.

A femur?

A mass of fleshy goo remained at the knob of the bone and the smell of the charred remains made the policemen gag.

They both gave each other a look of horror. Here in a town where the most serious crime would be a speeding ticket or jaywalking, the police were about to enter a whole world of horror beyond their wildest imagination.

CHAPTER ONE

Epping, New Hampshire.

Population = less than six thousand.

Epping is a rainy, small town that has been sarcastically nicknamed "The Center of the Universe". That has not stopped the residents from hosting parades, canoe races and music festivals. But when Sheila LaBarre arrived, the tiny hamlet soon became known for murder.

"She was a smart woman," forensic psychologist Paula Orange said. "Not book smart but intuitive. She could read people."

Sheila was born Sheila Kaye Bailey in Fort Payne, Alabama in 1958.

She was the youngest of six children. Her first marriage with a man named Ronnie Jennings would last less than two months. Jennings would find out that Sheila had been locking his child from a previous marriage in a closet to punish her. Jennings would divorce Sheila but she would find herself a new man in short order, tying the knot with John Baxter and moving to Chattanooga, Tennessee. Even though married, she would secretly fantasize about being swept away by a rich man. Sheila's mental illness would come to bear in her second marriage and that would end in divorce as well. Despondent, Sheila tried to kill herself and was sent to a psychiatric facility. She would be raped by an orderly inside the hospital.

Now single in Tennessee, the cash-strapped Sheila was forced to live in a local YMCA. She attended a church service and had a private talk with one of the preachers as she wanted "spiritual guidance." She would later claim that the reverend asked if she wanted to "sit in his lap." She then went to a psychiatrist who asked her if she had anal sex with any of her former husbands. The doctor then called Sheila at home and asked if "what she was wearing" and if she "was touching herself."

"If what we are to believe all of Sheila's stories," Orange said. "Then literally all of her interactions with men have ended with them as the pervert and her as the victim. Her sister would later testify that Sheila was molested by her father when she was young. Then her abusive marriages, the rape at the psych facility segues into a spiritual search where she meets a preacher who shows her the tent in his pants. Crazy."

CHAPTER TWO

Sheila turned to personal ads after her failures in marriage. She didn't like the normal courtship process of going to bars and meeting men there. She used the personal ads to cherry pick the men she wanted, men she could dominate.

"Whether on-line or off-line, Sheila behaved like a woman who was in complete control," Orange said. "She would develop a strange kind of power over men. It was almost as if she knew which men would be vulnerable to her feminine wiles and which ones would fight back. But when it came to Dr. Bill LaBarre, it was more of a case of getting the money."

While in Tennessee, Dr. LaBarre decided to take out a personal ad. He would get a response from Sheila who immediately sought to separate herself from the other paramours of the rich doctor.

She sent the doctor nude Polaroids of herself.

The strategy worked.

"She showed no shame in flirting with the older man and soon had him in the palm of her hand," Orange said. "He'd buy her fancy clothes, necklaces, the whole nine yards."

Wilfred "Bill" LaBarre was a successful chiropractor but lonely. Overweight and bespectacled, he had little to offer aside from his wealth. He was in his sixties and recently widowed.

Dr. Labarre was considered a good man by all who knew him. He had been the "Chiropractor of the Year" in 1983 but that would be the same year his beloved Edwina would pass away from cancer. Eager to salve the loneliness, he married another woman named Leona but she abandoned the doctor after a few years. He had two children from his first marriage; Laura and Gregory.

Now alone and widowed, the doctor wanted to spend his golden years enjoying his wealth.

And a young woman.

He would look at the nude Polaroids of the curvaceous Southern Belle, becoming obsessed.

"Here was a lonely, older man who all of a sudden had a 27-year old woman sending him nude photos. He thought he hit the jackpot."

Dr. LaBarre soon invited Sheila to come live with him at his farm in Epping, New Hampshire. The farm was a spacious one, a 115-acre horse ranch that according to LaBarre, "needed a female hand."

Sheila would become enamored by life on the farm, at least at first. She "never heard a June bug before" and the isolated country home gave her a peace that she never experienced.

Neighbors were not shocked that Dr. LaBarre took in such a younger woman as his girlfriend. He reportedly had other girlfriends after his wife died. "Sheila ran all the other girls off," one neighbor said.

But Sheila would prove to be a high-maintenance girlfriend. She would drain Dr. LaBarre's finances, making him buy her gifts and prizes which included a brand-new Silver Mercedes.

She also began to interject herself into LaBarre's estate and business dealings.

The farm that LaBarre owned was called the Old Harvey Farm. It was named after the original owners of the property who still lived in the area. But Sheila forced the doctor to change the name, she wanted it called something that reflected her personality.

The Silver Leopard Farm.

Sheila then had a sign made up and had it placed at the entrance.

She was marking her territory.

CHAPTER THREE

Despite the constant gifts and financial prizes, Sylvia proved to be an ungrateful sugar baby. The relationship would turn tempestuous after a few months. Sheila would claim that Dr. LaBarre often referred to himself as an "old fart" and looked the other way when Sheila began to have different men over for sex.

"He just worried about me when I would date far from home. But he was getting old and his heart would stop beating sometimes."

But the couple fought and police were routinely called to the residence to mediate their domestic disputes.

"You would sometimes hear gunshots," Bruce Allen, a LaBarre neighbor said. "You would hear her screaming, 'I'm going to kill you, you mother fucker!'"

Sheila once pulled a gun on the doctor and forced him out of the home. The chiropractor hid behind a boulder as his girlfriend shot at him.

LaBarre's daughter also recalled that she heard Sheila screaming threats at her father. "I'm gonna kill the horses and I'm going to kill you too."

Laura would later remark at how much her father changed after Sheila came into his life. He went from a normal, well-liked member of the community to a meek, submissive man.

"Sheila was all about being an opportunist," Orange said. "She had the ability to read a man, analyzing his weaknesses, size him up and then push the buttons. With LaBarre, she had a lonely man in front of her. He would tolerate anything in order not to lose her at first and then he simply became fearful of his life. These men in this small New England town did not have the wherewithal to deal with a violent sociopath like Sheila."

Sheila didn't stop with the renaming of Old Harvey Home. She soon took over the accounting duties at LaBarre's chiropractic business. She began organizing the practice into a well-oiled machine. She would track down patients who owed the doctor money and file numerous small claims in the Hampton District Court.

Concerned friends would advise him to dump Sheila before it was too late but it became apparent that the doctor either didn't know how or was afraid to. Dr. LaBarre informed neighbor Bruce Allen that he "had to get rid of her" and that he wanted to "send her back to Alabama. Hopefully, she'll stay there."

Her power over Dr. LaBarre increased to the point where he had given her power of attorney. She began rewriting his will, becoming the executor of his estate. The will stated that he was leaving everything to "a very special lady known as Sheila Kaye Jennings LaBarre."

"The will was very carefully redacted from the original," Orange said. "She kept a lot of the parts of the original and used her own typewriter to amend the little detail of where all the assets will go to. She was very astute and covered her tracks very well for someone who was supposedly schizophrenic."

The two would live together (Sheila would move out briefly but claim to be his common-law wife) from 1987 until LaBarre's death in 2000 at the age of 74. The coroner logged his cause of death as heart disease. There were suspicions among those close to the doctor that believe Sheila poisoned him to hasten the process.

"He was pretty old," Orange said. "And according to the autopsy, the heart disease was significant. So Sheila didn't have anything to do with his death despite the suspicions. The killings would come later."

Sheila would inherit the farm, LaBarre's Chiropractor office, two apartments and a rental home.

This was all valued at over two million dollars in assets.

Strangely, Sheila would marry a Jamaican national named Wayne Ennis in August of 1995 while living with Dr. LaBarre. Ennis drove a tour bus around Jamaica and Sheila made sure that when she toured the islands with Dr. LaBarre that they would cross paths with her Jamaican lover. She arranged for Ennis to obtain a visa and took him back to the farm with her. She would later claim that she and the doctor had stopped having sex and that she "had needs" which apparently Ennis took care of. She would later concede to pleasing the doctor sexually, "I'd use my hand," she said afterward.

Ennis would live in the farmhouse for almost a year. He had his own numerous encounters with Sheila which were violent and bizarre. One night, she ordered him to get in the car. The two then drove around the quiet town, Sheila's voice taking on a conspiratorial tone.

"I wish one of those damn horses would just kick him (Dr. LaBarre) in the head," Sheila said. "Kick him in the head and kill his old ass. I've thought about strangling him myself. But now I have a better idea. I want you to kill him."

Ennis was too frightened to say no to Sheila. The two would eventually divorce and the court records reveal that Sheila took out a restraining order against him.

Ennis disputed the allegations and stated that Sheila was the abuser.

He would later recall being punched, pushed, and shot at by Sheila.

"She told me that she was going to send me back to Jamaica in a box," Ennis said.

Dr. LaBarre told Ennis that Sheila was crazy and believed that she would eventually kill him. He gave the Jamaican money and sent him to the bus station, requesting that he leave town for his own safety.

After the relationship with Ennis ended, Sheila began dating James Brackett.

She and James would remain together for six years despite the fact that Sheila would attack Brackett with a pair of scissors, a machete, and an ax. When all of that failed she tried to shoot him.

The two would break up after which Brackett would get himself a vanity license plate that read "I'm Alive."

Brackett recalled moments where Sheila would act sweet and nice only to go into a violent rage moments later. He said that the greatest example was a time when he was taking a long bath with Sheila only to have her get out of the tub and smash him in the face with a two-foot grill brush.

Two of his teeth would be knocked out from the impact.

Sheila would attack Brackett for a variety of transgressions that would not be guilty of. Hurting her rabbits, damaging her property or having affairs with other women.

Brackett finally had enough, escaping from the farm on one rainy night and hitchhiking back into town.

"I'm lucky to be alive," he would later state.

CHAPTER FOUR

Sheila inherited the farm after LaBarre's death. The doctor's children tried to contest the will but were told that the odds of winning the case were 50/50 at best. They would also have to front over $50,000 to pay for the court costs.

Sheila soon turned the farm into her own private fiefdom. She would hire young men to help her around the place then pay them with her sexual favors or sometimes just beat the shit out of them.

"There would neighbors that would claim to see young men leave her house," Orange said. "They would look beaten up; black eyes, bloody lips, facial contusions. God knows what else."

Her neighbors began to suspect something fishy was going on but had no real evidence to call the police with.

"The first time I met Sheila LaBarre was at the Harvey Farm Stand," said Bonnie Meroth, one of Sheila's neighbors. "It was during the summertime when the produce was ready. I had no basic interaction with her except that of someone standing next to another person as a consumer. And she suddenly turned around and said 'I'll kill you if you come down to my farm' or words to that effect."

Bonnie would later claim that Sheila would try to scare her while driving down the road, nearly running her over while she was on her morning walk.

When she wasn't intimidating neighbors and townsfolk, Sheila would use the farm as the playground for her own private fetishes.

She liked to control and bully men. Stroking one of her pet rabbits, she would punish and insult the men unlucky enough to work at her farm.

"Are you kidding me?" Sheila yelled at the young man who dropped the wheelbarrow. "This should have been done yesterday."

He was young and naive, needing money. If it meant taking lip from Sheila, so be it. He needed work and she seemed nice when she hired him.

"Hurry up!" Sheila said, kicking the man in his buttocks. "Move, move. Are you kidding me? I've never seen a lazier man in my life."

Fatigued after working sixteen hours for seven days straight, the young man keeled over in exhaustion, dropping the wheelbarrow.

"Bitch made, perverted ass pedophile!" Sheila said. "Is this what I am paying you for? I am paying you to work. Now get off your bitch ass. Now!"

It became apparent that Sheila had a gift. A gift of controlling a certain type of man. Verbally abusive and overbearing, she encountered very little resistance.

She kicked the young man again. "Your name is 'bitch', you hear me?"

His real name was Michael Deloge.

CHAPTER FIVE

Deloge had problems as a teen. He got caught up in drugs and found himself on the streets, living out of homeless shelters. In 2004, he would meet Sheila LaBarre.

Deloge became smitten with the woman whom he saw as the life of the party. She would drink beer and play country songs on a guitar. According to Deloge's stepfather, Gordon Boston, the duo would indulge in drugs and study "sadistic material".

Deloge would join Sheila at her farm and soon become her personal whipping boy. Sheila would slap him around like a rag doll. One of the fellow ranch hands, Philip Sullos, recalled witnessing Sheila beating on Deloge with a hardwood stick until he bled. Deloge cowered and took the beating. She would then throw Deloge into a windowless shack and slam the door shut.

Deloge would cower meekly in the corner until Sheila came and got him, making no attempt to escape.

He would be declared missing in 2004 and no one would ever see him again.

In February of 2006, Sheila began looking for a new farmhand. She had her own criteria. He had to be young but pliable to her controlling methods.

She would find the perfect foil in Kenny Countie.

"Kenny was a lovely boy," Carolynn Lodge, Kenny's mother said. "He couldn't do enough for you. Everyone was his friend. I was so proud of him. He never had a horrible word for anybody and that was the problem. He trusted everybody."

Kenny's trust would lead him into Sheila LaBarre's trap.

Kenny would answer one of Sheila's personal ads. The young man was still naive and according to some reports had a "low IQ". The two met through a telephone personal ad service with Sheila calling up the young man and charming him in a way that no woman ever did.

"He (Kenny) told my son Brian that he met a 47-year old woman in New Hampshire," Lodge said. "She owned a farm. She owned a beautiful car. And she was rich. And he was serious about her."

"Kenny fit Sheila's psychological criteria," Orange said. "She targeted men whom she could overpower not only physically but also mentally. She was older than Kenny and light years more cunning. She knows exactly what to say and do to push his buttons. She takes the lead, telling him that he is going to be 'in for the time of his life' and that she 'can't wait to see him.' To a young man with limited experience and intelligence like Kenny, this is music to his ears."

Sheila would arrive at Kenny's home in the silver Mercedes. The silver leopard, the cougar, picking up her prey and taking him back to her lair.

Kenny's family would never see him again.

Sheila would use the same methods on Kenny as she did on the men in the past. She seduced the young man first then isolated him in her farmhouse. Then she berated him verbally before beating the shit out of him with face slaps, punches, and a wooden stick.

The beatings would come to a head during a weekend in February of 2000. Sheila beat Kenny's face into a pulp, took the wooden cane to his legs and may have poisoned him.

Then she decided to take him shopping at Walmart.

Placing him in a wheelchair, she rolled him around the outlet as she stocked up on garden supplies. She dumped two containers of diesel fuel into the prone Kenny's lap.

Little did he know that she would later use the gas to incinerate his body.

Customers gawked at the odd couple, concerned about the contusions on Kenny's face.

"Fuck you looking at?" Sheila would scream as she sped down through the aisle.

Employees of the store soon became concerned, calling the police.

The cops would arrive, confronting the couple in the store. They inquired about Kenny's condition but he didn't respond. Instead, Sheila took the lead, telling Kenny that he "didn't have to talk to these assholes."

The police didn't follow through. Kenny remained silent as Sheila rolled him through the store and out the door. No crime had been witnessed and they let the couple go.

Kenny's mother would later sue the police for negligence but it was tossed out of court in 2010.

A few nights after the Walmart incident, Sheila would make a frantic phone call to the police.

"I got a pervert in my house!" she screamed into the phone. "He's a pedophile! A pedophile!"

In a bizarre sequence of events, Sheila began to play a recording for the detective on the other end. She had routinely audio recorded everything she did, trying to incriminate the young men she worked with into admitting they were pedophiles. On this occasion, she played back a recording of her and Kenny.

"On the tape was my son, vomiting," Lodge said. "He kept saying 'he's faking, he's faking.'"

Sheila would ask Kenny if he was a pedophile on the tape. Kenny would answer 'yes'.

"Now he's a pedophile," Kenny's mother said. "Now he's raping children. Raping his brother. He's vomiting."

The police would write off the call as the rantings of a schizophrenic. They did not immediately respond to the residence.

Sheila would then kill Kenny Countie.

"She had to justify the killing of the young men in her own mind," Orange said. "For some bizarre reason, she would brainwash herself into thinking that her victims were pedophiles. She would repeat the question like a mantra, 'Are you a pedophile? Are you a pedophile?' Working herself up into an angry and violent state of mind before she killed the man."

Sheila's sister, Lynn Noojin, believed that Sheila was sexually abused by her father. Because of this, she became obsessed with child molestation. She would accuse the young men that worked for her of various sexual deviations, including pedophilia, incest, and bestiality.

CHAPTER SIX

After the bizarre call to police, authorities would not arrive at the farmhouse until the next morning. The police would enter the grounds, seeing both the burning mattress and barrel with Kenny's remains. They would not identify the burning bones as belonging to Kenny until much later.

Sheila had murdered Kenny the night before. She attacked Kenny ferociously with a kitchen knife, pushing the already weakened young man to the floor and stabbing away.

Blood sprayed and splattered everywhere.

Sheila then dragged Kenny's body out to her yard where she doused his body with the diesel fuel they had purchased at Walmart.

Lighting a match, she set the dead man on fire. She then took her pet rabbit in her lap, pulled up a chair and watched Kenny Countie burn.

"He was dismembered," Kenny's mother said, fighting tears. "And he was put in a pit and burned. But my son, he just wanted to be loved. I can't imagine what he must have been thinking. Because he was all alone."

Police would look throughout the house and find blood splatter on the walls and floor. A forensic team arrived and matched the blood with Kenny's DNA sample from his Army days. They would find the wallet of Michael Deloge but not his body.

Hundreds of police would spend seventeen days searching the 115-acre property. They found numerous burn pits and blood remains that were so old they had layers of dust on them. They would find clothing that belonged to Deloge and some toes that remain unidentified (it is rumored that the toes may belong to a mysterious Irish man who Sheila claims was stalking her.)

Going on the run from the cops, Sheila hitchhiked along Interstate 293. She was then picked up by Stephen Martello.

"Thanks so much for stopping," Sheila said.

"No problem," Martello said, looking the buxom Southern Belle up and down. His heart began to race.

Will he get lucky?

"My car broke down about two miles back. I got into a fight with my boyfriend and I'm trying to get to Dorchester."

"I'm headed that way," Martello said.

Sheila clutched her purse as if it were a security blanket and she kept looking back at the rear window.

"You all right?" he asked.

"Yeah," Sheila said "Just a little rattled. You know, it has been a tough day."

Martello took Sheila to the drug store when she said she needed to stop off and "buy some things". He tailed Sheila around the store until she bought a douche. Noting her erratic behavior, Martello disappeared out of Sheila's earshot to call the police on his cell phone.

"Hi," Martello said. "Just curious if you folks are looking for someone who just robbed a bank or an escaped mental patient. I just met a woman who is acting kind of strange."

When the authorities informed him that they were not actively investigating someone with that kind of background, Martello took Sheila to a hotel room.

The two would engage in wild and loud sex.

"You just had sex with an angel," Sheila proclaimed after they were done.

"Is that right?"

"You're not like the other men," Sheila said. "My boyfriend, Jesus, I just caught him with a huge stack of child porn. He is a pedophile. So are all those damn cops. Pedophiles, all of them. I think all sex offenders must die."

Martello said nothing. Instead, he put his pants and shoes on as fast as he could as Sheila continued to go on another bizarre rant.

"Vengeance is mine saith the Lord," Sheila said, laying on the bed in post-coital repose. "I was sent back to earth as an angel. I know how to speak to God in Hebrew. Do it every night."

Martello excused himself and high-tailed it out of the hotel room. He arrived home and saw the television broadcast about Sheila. He didn't call the police, worried that he would be an accessory to her crimes. Instead, Martello drove to the station and practically sprinted to the front desk.

"I think I just met Sheila LaBarre."

"To the end, Sheila had control over just about every man put in front of her," Orange said. "Here was a guy who picks her up at the side of the road. He thinks she is crazy enough to where he calls the cops to find out if there are any missing mental patients. He knows that she has a screw loose but he has sex with her anyway. It may be a poor reflection on men for sure but his response is typical. The men that Sheila encountered, from Dr. LaBarre all the way to Stephen Martello, all had the same false narratives going on in their head. They did not see a beautiful woman as something evil. It just didn't fit their narrative. So when Sheila begins her abuse, they just can't believe it. They refuse to hit a 'woman' back. She gets them 'pussy whipped' then beats the shit out of them. Rinse and repeat."

Sheila LaBarre would later be arrested for the murders of Michael Deloge and Kenneth Countje. She would plead no guilty on the grounds of insanity.

"This is a sick, sick woman," her attorney would argue. "Deeply disturbed."

Court-appointed psychiatrists would agree, testifying that Sheila was delusional as well as schizophrenic.

The jury would visit both LaBarre's farm and the Walmart where she frequented first hand. Sheila would join them as well although she was forced to wear a stun belt.

The jury did not buy her insanity defense and found her guilty.

"The fact that she has to remain for the rest of her life behind bars," Kenny's mother said. "She got what she asked for. She'll never see the light of day. Horrible thing is that my son, he's not here with me. He was only twenty-four."

Sheila LaBarre is now serving life in without possibility of parole.

KILLER CON WOMAN : THE TRUE STORY OF DEE DEE MOORE

28

SUSAN GRAHAM

Abraham Shakespeare didn't have too much going on in life. He was the son of an orange picker limited to menial day jobs. He never held a job where he made more than eight dollars an hour.

He didn't have a car, a driver's license or a credit card. He dropped out of school and could barely read or write.

The lanky 6'5" inch, 190 lbs laborer would patrol around town, looking for something to steal or people to assault.

He would go to jail two times and when he was released in 1995, he went to live with his mother.

Trying to cobble together any kind of life, Abraham would find work as a garbage man. Then he worked in a restaurant washing dishes before gaining employment on a shipping and receiving dock.

He was on the road to nowhere unless he hit the lottery.

On November 15th, 2006, however, he did just that. He rode shotgun with a truck driver named Michael Ford. They were making meat deliveries to restaurants in the area.

Ford then stopped off at the Town Star mini-mart in Frostproof. Abraham stayed in the car and Ford asked if he wanted anything.

Abraham only had ten dollars in his pocket. He asked for two quick picks in the lotto drawing.

Ford would buy the winning ticket for Abraham. The numbers 6, 12, 13, 34, 42, and 52 netted Abraham the $30 million dollar jackpot.

Ford would then sue him for what he believed should be "his share of the proceeds". He wanted no less than $1 million dollars and later claimed that Abraham had stolen the two tickets from his wallet.

"He knows the truth," Abraham said of Ford. "I know the truth."

The lawsuit hit the news wires but it took the jury only an hour to rule that Abraham did not steal the winning ticket from Ford's wallet.

"From my background investigation, he (Abraham) was always kind of a transient type," Ford's attorney, Michael Laurato, said. "If it wasn't for his criminal record, he kind of didn't exist."

Abraham would elect to take the lump sum cash payment of $17 million instead of the thirty annual payments totaling $30 million.

LET THE PARTY BEGIN

"Abraham was suddenly given the keys to the good life," Miami journalist Zack Jacobs said. "He threw a big party and suddenly found himself surrounded by numerous hangers-on. They partied and wined and dined. He paid them back for their attention with lavish gifts and cash prizes."

The first thing Abraham did was pay off his back child support which totaled almost $9,000. He then placed $1 million dollars into a trust fund for his son. He then gave his stepfather $1 million dollars and his three step-sisters $250,000 apiece. But his generosity didn't stop with his family. He paid off a $185,000 mortgage for a friend, $60,000 for another friend and another $53,000 for a mortgage for a man he had been "knowing for years."

Word of Abraham's open wallet began to spread.

His brother's best friend came over and he gave him $40,000. He gave his mother $12,000 and his sister $10,000.

In other words, he became the family ATM.

"Abraham's mother was the only one who grew wary of all of the well-wishers," Jacobs said. "She worked in a cafeteria at the local junior college and was a church-going woman. She thought that money was evil and was leery of Abraham getting so much of it. She knew that the folks coming around were just doing it out of their own selfish desires. They all wanted something from Abraham whereas before they wouldn't even give him the time of day."

Abraham would not heed his mother's warnings. He would write checks to whoever tugged at his heart strings. This meant paying for funerals of loved ones and people he didn't know.

"Abraham really had no idea of the value of money," Jacobs said. "And that isn't an insult. Remember, here was a guy who was in and out of jail. He never made more than eight dollars an hour. So, in his mind, seventeen million dollars would last forever. So, I think like most lottery winners, the initial euphoria simply consumed him. He was not thinking annuities and investments. He was simply enjoying all the indulgences and attention money could buy."

Abraham had other ideas about money.

"The Bible states it's better to give than to receive," Abraham said, explaining his gift giving.

Arnold Levine, another attorney who represented Ford in the suit, described Abraham as an "angry guy" whose made sure that his gifts came with "strings attached."

"My sense," Levine said, "was that some of his family members were unhappy with the amount of money he had parceled out to them. Were there people who were jealous? I would assume so."

After he gifted his relatives, Abraham began indulging himself. He purchased a Nissan Altima and a Rolex watch from a pawnshop. He then bought a 2006 F-150 pickup, a 2007 BMW 750i and finally a $1.1 million dollar home.

The brick and stucco home came replete with security cameras and a gate. It was over 6,500 square feet with an enclosed pool and a two two-car garages.

Aside from these extravagances, Abraham regretted winning the lottery. He was subject to constant requests for money from friends and even people he didn't know.

"I'd have been better off broke," Abraham later said to his brother. He then confided to another friend that "I thought all these people were my friends, but then I realized all they want is just money."

But Abraham only saw the tip of the iceberg. He was about to meet someone who didn't just want a little of his money. She wanted all of it.

And she was willing to kill him to get it.

Her name was Dorice Donegan Moore, better known as "Dee Dee".

ENTER THE CON

Dee Dee was a self-styled entrepreneur. A tall and shapely blonde, she was thirty-five years old and had a twenty-six-year-old boyfriend.

"Dee Dee was the kind of psychopath that could focus on her mark and not take no for an answer," Jacobs said. "She had an over the top, type-A personality. She could make her mark feel as if they were the only person in the world that mattered. She could look you straight in the eye and lie without any compunction."

She read about Abraham's story in the paper and the wheels in her head began to turn.

Dee Dee Morgan had tried to meet Abraham through his friends and even called his mother to no avail. Finally, she found out who sold him the million dollar estate, a realtor named Barbara Jackson.

"When I met her (Dee Dee), she was in a wheelchair," Jackson said. "She said she was in a car accident."

Dee Dee listened as Jackson told others about Abraham and how he changed their outlook about money. He insisted that it wasn't about money at all. It was about helping people. Jackson encouraged others to embrace this similar outlook.

Dee Dee feigned interest as she introduced herself to Jackson, telling the realtor that she was a writer. She said that she wanted to write an article or maybe even a book about Abraham, documenting his life so far and his viewpoints about money.

Jackson acquiesced and arranged for Dee Dee to meet Abraham.

"When she came to the house," Jackson said, "She jumped out of a Hummer, walking. And she was on heels. She said she healed herself through scuba therapy. It wasn't even two weeks."

Both Jackson and Abraham listened to Dee Dee's spiel. She spoke of her admiration for Abraham's philanthropy and wanted the world to hear about it.

Abraham was naïve and fell for the con. He agreed to have Dee Dee do the story about him.

"Abraham was vulnerable to someone with the manipulative charm of Dee Dee," Jacobs said. "Here was a guy who was about as down on his luck as you can get. Then he is a multi-millionaire overnight. He gets all the attention and love that was denied him his whole life. He really didn't know who to trust. Then along comes Dee Dee. She's well-spoken, well-dressed and seems to know what's going on inside his head."

What neither Abraham or Jackson didn't know was that Dee Dee Moore had a history of con artistry.

She had once staged a hoax that she believed would enable her to keep a Lincoln Navigator which was about to be repossessed. She had fallen hopelessly behind on the payments and had someone put the car in a garage. She then pretended that she was carjacked, kidnapped and raped by "three Mexican guys."

Dee Dee went all out in the pre-meditated scheme. She taped her wrists and threw herself out of someone else's moving car to make her injuries look real.

"This was an elaborate ruse," Jacobs said. "She had a friend drive her down the highway and she propelled herself out of the vehicle. She then tore apart her own clothes, smeared her make-up and started to cry. All of this was done as she crawled down the side of the highway, waiting for a sympathetic motorist to come pick her up."

A Good Samaritan would come along and take her to the hospital. She detailed her story to the police and medical staff, even going so far as to take a rape exam.

But her scheme was exposed and she would plead no contest to the charge and get probation. Always on the make for a new mark, Dee Dee needed another scheme. When she read about the lottery winning Abraham and his lawsuit with Ford, she had found herself a new patsy.

"Dee Dee couldn't make it on the straight road," Jacobs said. "Her businesses, whatever she was doing, were not generating any sufficient revenue for her to maintain the lifestyle that she felt she was entitled to.

So she had to swindle and con. Unfortunately for Abraham, he got in her crosshairs."

LET'S START A BUSINESS

"Dee Dee was a master manipulator," Jacobs said. "She befriended Abraham first and gained his trust. She picked up on the fact that he had all of these people after his money. So she did some reverse psychology on him. She convinced Abraham that she was the opposite, that she would never take anything from him."

Convinced of Dee Dee's trustworthiness, Abraham agreed to start an LLC with the woman. They titled the business "Abraham Shakespeare LLC".

"He agreed to do this under the provision that anyone who asked for money would have to go through her," Jacobs said. "She convinced him that she had his best interests in mind. But in her mind, she saw him as a dupe. A rube. She was telling herself 'I'm going to work this guy. I'm going to work this guy and take everything he has. Schmuck!'"

The corporation was in Abraham's name but the funds were under the control of Dee Dee.

Once she had control of the LLC, Dee Dee proceeded to withdraw $1 million dollars.

"She had totally hoodwinked poor Abraham," Jacobs said. "Now everything was under her own company banner, some type of bullshit medical company. Nothing came out of Abraham's account without her signature."

Abraham had stopped giving money to people without recompense. He then became the town ATM around his native Plant City. Judy Haggins helped him keep track of the loans as to who owed what.

Judy knew Abraham for fifteen years and she was taken aback that Dee Dee was involving herself in Abraham's affairs.

"When Abraham got ready to go to the bank one day to see about his money, (Moore) immediately called me on the phone," Judy said in the recording of her conversation with Smith. "You've got to stall him, Judy. He can't go to the bank."

Judy then received money from Abraham's account to pay for her help. "It was a little bit of money for me. (Moore) felt like Abraham should pay me to take his mama. Abraham used to come to me and say, 'Now you know that white woman got my money, she can do anything to me.' I said, 'Abraham, you can go get your money.'"

Judy could not stall Abraham, however. He drove over to Dee Dee's home to confront her. He wanted his money back under his name. All of it.

"It isn't working out," Abraham said. "I am going to the bank and straighten this shit out."

Dee Dee did her best to try and talk him out of it but Abraham was resolute in his decision.

"This was her worst fear come to light," Jacobs said. "Her mark had figured her out. Abraham was being nice about it but if he went to the bank there would be a huge investigation. She would go to jail. She couldn't let that happen."

Dee Dee would play along and told Abraham that she had all of his money in a safe she had behind her desk. She walked over to the safe and opened it.

But none of Abraham's money inside.

The only thing she had inside was a gun.

Spinning around, she pointed the pistol at Abraham.

"Aw shit," Abraham said. "Don't do it."

Dee Dee didn't listen. She fired twice, hitting Abraham in his chest, killing him. She then rolled up his body in a tarp and stole his cell phone.

"Her idea was to tap into people who owed Abraham money," Jacobs said. "She scanned through all of Abraham's text messages and realized how many people owed him money. Close to three million dollars. She figured she could impersonate him via cell phone messages and collect on these debts. An insane plan to any rational human being. But to do Dee Dee, a psychopath who thought she was smarter than everyone, it looked like easy money."

CLEANING UP THE MESS

Dee Dee contacted her ex-husband, James Moore to do some "yard work". She asked if he could dig a hole in her yard in April of 2009.

James could only scratch his head at the odd request.

"Why?" James asked.

"Oh, I just need a hole to bury some concrete and trash in," Dee Dee said. "I don't want my landlord to see all the stuff out here."

James would dig the hole then leave. But Dee Dee would call him back two hours later, however, asking him to fill the hole.

James, who was paid to do yard work by Dee Dee, agreed to fill the hole but didn't see what she had placed inside as it was now dark.

Dee Dee had placed Abraham's body in the hole.

A BLOOD TRAIL

Dee Dee continued to cover her tracks. She stole Abraham's cell phone and sent text messages to his family and friends, pretending to be the man she had just killed.

"Have to get away for awhile," Dee Dee texted Abraham's mother under his own cell phone number. "Going to the Caribbean."

The people receiving the texts became suspicious, however, because the texts didn't sound like him. Abraham was functionally illiterate. They would then text back for clarification and would be ignored. His mother grew especially worried. She texted back and told Abraham to call her.

His family now stalled, Dee Dee turned her attention to Abraham's assets. She used her own company, American Medical Professionals, to purchase Abraham's home.

In February of 2009, Dee Dee would purchase a 2008 Corvette for her boyfriend for $70,000. She would pay for this vehicle with a cashier's check from her American Medical Professionals, LLC business account.

"She had a boy toy," Jacobs said. "And she lavished the kid with money that she stole from Abraham. This included a house and a Corvette."

The following month, she purchased a 2009 Hummer for herself for $90,000 before taking her boy toy on a luxury vacation.

Abraham's family would report him missing on November 9th of 2009, almost seven months after his presumed date of death.

"Abraham told a friend that he was tired," Jacobs said. "He was tired of people constantly pressing him for money. So he hinted to more than one friend that he was 'fittin' to get outta here.' When no one saw him for a long period of time, they just wrote it off to the fact that he had gotten fed up with the situation and left town. It was only after they had not seen him for such a prolonged period of time that they finally reported it."

When questioned by police, Dee stated that Abraham left town. She said he was either in Texas, Jamaica, Puerto Rico, Florida or was admitted into a hospital.

"He was sick of people asking him for money," Dee Dee said. "I helped him leave town. He didn't tell me where he was going."

Dee Dee would state that the reason Abraham was taken off the account was because he didn't want to pay taxes. She couldn't give a reason for the fact that over $1 million was withdrawn only days after his name was taken off the LLC listing. She then said that Abraham also didn't want to pay child support.

Thinking she needed more accomplices, Dee Dee thought she could buy some. She approached the mother of one of Abraham's sons, telling her that she would give her a $200,000 house if she would lie to detectives and tell them that she had seen Abraham in recent days. She then paid a cousin of Abraham, Cedric Edom, over $5,000 to send his mother a birthday card and imply that it was from Abraham.

Abraham had not contacted his family since April of 2009. They believed that he was off on a Caribbean island somewhere enjoying his money.

"On a cruise," Dee Dee texted through Abraham's cell phone. "Having a great time."

But Abraham was far from the Jamaican isles. He was buried in five feet of dirt under a concrete slab.

LEAVING FINGERPRINTS BEHIND

Dee Dee sold her Hummer to a friend of a Chevrolet dealer for only $49,000. She said that she needed to get quick cash. Three weeks later, she had lunch with Elizabeth Walker, Abraham's mother.

Dee Dee also typed up a letter which she wanted to pass off as coming from Abraham.

"She had a brand-new laptop, set up and a printer, (and) she had a rubber-type gloves on," Abraham's friend, Gregory Smith recalled. "And a scarf pullover-type thing over her head."

'Don't worry about Dee,' the letter read. 'There are too many people that know I left. I gave her enough money... she would not take anything from me unless I agreed.'

She then had Gregory call Abraham's mother and pretend he was Abraham.

"Hi Mom," Gregory said. "I'm fine. Had to get away."

"Who is this?" Elizabeth said. "You're not Abe! Who are you?"

Dee Dee made her first strategic error here. Elizabeth Walker knew her son's voice and the voice on the other end did not belong to him. She contacted police who investigated and eventually caught up with Gregory Smith.

Gregory would cooperate and play informant against Dee Dee. This would involve the use of an undercover police officer to aid Gregory.

Dee Dee had told Gregory that she needed someone to take the fall for Abraham's murder. She told Gregory to find someone that would accept $50,000 in exchange for declaring themselves guilty of Abraham's murder. Gregory told the investigators of the scheme and they had an undercover cop, Mike Smith, come along with Gregory as they arranged a deal.

"I did it (help the undercover operation) because when they explained to me what was going on and they said they had their suspicions that something like I told them," Gregory Smith said. "He had money. He could have went anywhere. Anybody was saying anything. I didn't know where he was, really didn't go into where he was. But the deal is when they came to me and they explained to me that there was an investigation going on. And I wouldn't get in no trouble and I could walk out of there right now, but they needed some help to find Abraham. I said I'd see what I could do. "

Dee Dee met with the undercover officer. The con artist was about to be conned.

"The undercover officer explained himself as someone up on federal charges," Jacobs said. "He was about to be sent to jail for life. He could take the $50,000 and live it up in his final days. But what he needed from Dee Dee was proof that he was the killer."

Dee Dee took the bait. She showed the undercover detective where she had buried Abraham, five feet under a concrete slab in her backyard.

"I need you to dig him up," Dee Dee said. "And then burn his body."

She also gave the undercover cop the gun that was used to kill Abraham.

"She gave Mike the map of her backyard," Jacobs said. "She was so blinded by her own need to get away with the crime that she didn't she that she was being played. He was wired up the whole time. They had everything they needed on tape. She confessed to everything."

"Don't forget to bring the marshmallows," Dee Dee said to the undercover cop when she told him to burn Abraham's body.

EXCAVATING THE BODY

Digging at the site, the police unearthed Abraham's body. They then brought Dee Dee back in for another interrogation.

The con woman would give them multiple stories. First, she said that drug dealers killed Abraham. Then it was his attorney that had him killed. Then she would blame her fourteen-year-old son before finally saying that she killed Abraham herself...but only in self-defense.

Dee Dee's manipulations didn't stop there.

She told one of the investigating detectives, David Clark, that she hoped they could eventually have sex once the investigation was over.

"I find you very attractive," Dee Dee said to Clark.

Detectives would estimate that Abraham died around April 6th or 7th. They would take Dee Dee into custody and charge her with accessory to murder.

"The money was like a curse to him," Dee Dee said to reporters. "And now it's become a curse to me. God knows I would never take another human being's life."

COURTROOM DRAMA

During the trial, Dee Dee began making threats to jurors. Two of the jurors would state that Gregory Smith had intimidated them in the parking lot. Smith, a convicted felon five times over, denied the charges. The judge would ask one of the jurors if she had felt threatened by Dee Dee or any members of her family or friends and the juror simply responded that she wanted to feel safe.

The judge would then caution Dee Dee from making 'facial expressions' at the jurors as she would stare stone-faced at some of them, trying to intimidate.

The jury would deliberate for three hours before finding Moore guilty of the first-degree murder charge.

"She got every bit of his money," Assistant State Attorney Jay Pruner said. "He found out about it and threatened to kill her. She killed him first."

Dee Dee's attorney Byron Hileman argued otherwise, stating that there were other suspects that the prosecution should have went after.

"There were a lot of people who owed Mr. Shakespeare a lot of money," Hileman said. "One guy owed him a million dollars. The police focused on Dee Dee Moore and they didn't even consider other people."

Judge Emmett Battles called Dee Dee "the most manipulative person I have ever seen" and that she was "cold, calculating and cruel."

Dee Dee Moore would be convicted of first-degree murder on December 20th, 2012.

She would be sentenced to life in prison without the possibility of parole with an additional 25 years.

"'I'm missing my little brother," Abraham's brother Robert Brown said after the proceedings. "What ain't gonna be back no more. Dead and gone, and everything. He ain't coming back."

Dee Dee maintains that she is innocent and that her trial did not have evidence that would have exonerated her. She states that she is writing two books as well as penning poetry.

"Friends are a gift,
You give yourself.
When life has too many,
Mountains to climb alone." - Dee Dee Moore

bonus story:

"Why is this happening?"

Those may have been Greg Hosa's last audible words as Andrew Flentjar and Stacy Lea-Caton brutally forced him to the ground. The answer Flentjar gave would shock not just Hosa, but both of his attackers. For it was that response that would have allowed both Flentjar and Lea-Caton to realize that they were not part of the just cause they had believed themselves to be, but were in fact at the mercy of Kim Snibson's deluded and volatile plan.

Kim Snibson is a master manipulator who was envious of the life Greg Hosa and his wife Kathryn McKay had built together. Most notably, their horse farm. Situated in Nowra, New South Wales, Champagne Shires would be considered a small property when compared to the amount of land horse farms usually covered. Still, despite its modest size, it was far grander that Snibson could ever hope to own herself. For her, Champagne Shires was the perfect combination of all her fondest desires and life passions. Living next door to her dream made reality, it didn't take long for her fantasies of owning the property to become a perceived right. Snibson's greed led her to believe that she deserved Champagne Shires, while her ego convinced her that she could have it, if only the current owners were dealt away with.

Once Hosa and McKay had agreed to stable her horse, Snibson had the perfect excuse to visit her neighbors. She would come by often and grew to know both Hosa and McKay well. This access only fuelled her lust for the property and her disdain for the happy owners. Unaware of Snibson's feelings towards them, Hosa and McKay remained kind and generous to their neighbor. On one known occasion, Snibson had fallen behind in payments and owed the couple $300 for the care of her horse. Hosa and McKay had agreed to continue to stable her horse and told Snibson that she could pay them when she was able. This generosity did not provoke gratitude in Snibson, but instead fed into her increasing resentment. By this time she had begun to believe that she could force the couple to sign over the rights to Champagne Shires to her, kill them, and live happily on the property without consequence. Rationally this plan is ludicrous, but given her past success, Snibson believed it to be perfect.

Years earlier Snibson had inherited her house in Calymea Street, Nowra Hill, from an elderly woman named Judith Plankas. It was this property that had made her a neighbor of Hosa and McKay, and ultimately, it was in this house that the couple would be murdered. But it wasn't until after her arrest that questions began to arise as to exactly why and how Ms Plankas came to deed the property to Snibson.

In an interview with Take-5 Magazine, Snibson's ex-husband recalled how Ms Snibson had befriended Ms Plankas. At the time, the elderly dog breeder had been diagnosed with cancer and had needed help taking care of her animals. Snibson had been quick to offer assistance and for a while must have struck the sickly Ms Plankas as a Godsend. But, as Mr Snibson told Take-5 Magazine, "Kim got hold of powerful tranquilizers and quietly killed the older dogs." Perhaps accustomed to Kim's crueler actions, or blinded by devotion, it is believed that Mr Snibson neglected to inform Plankas of what Kim had done. By all appearances, Ms Plankas had no idea what kind of woman she had welcomed into her home.

"Then on April 17, 2003," Mr Snibson recalled, "Judith's condition suddenly worsened. She changed her will that night, leaving the house to Kim, and died the next day."

This would not be the first time Mr Snibson had been privy to the threat Kim posed to those around her. And it would not be the only time his failure to believe or act lead to disastrous consequences. In the same interview, he revealed a conversation he had once had with a woman named Rebecca. She had only been 15-years-old when Ms Snibson had convinced her to move out of the home and in with the Snibson family.

"We've got a free babysitter," Ms Snibson had announced when she had brought the teenager home, according to her ex-husband. He went on to say that, "later, Rebecca sought me out and what she had to say rocked me. Kim had kept a horse at a stable owned by an elderly couple and Rebecca said (that Kim) talked about tying them up, making them sign over their property to her and killing them."

Still, it would seem that Mr Snibson was not then willing to believe his wife capable of such things. But Rebecca wasn't Snibson's first nor only attempt at recruiting accomplices in her murder plot. Nor was the teenager's confession the only one to be dismissed. Armed with vicious lies and a willingness to manipulate all those around her, Snibson approached numerous people. Perhaps it is a testament to her skill at manipulation, or her ability to choose those reluctant to cause a stir without any solid evidence, but many of the people she approached never spoke of the conversations until after she had been arrested. Mr Snibson claimed that was when he began to receive calls from dozens of friends, most of which started with 'I've been wanting to tell you this for years'.

"Then they'd tell me about an affair she'd had or how she'd tried to enlist them in a desperate scheme to have someone beaten up or killed," he told Take-5 Magazine. He also spoke about how a friend had told him that 'Kim had wanted an old lady beaten up because she said her son had molested one of your girls'. "Nobody has touched my daughters," Mr Snibson said. "It was a fantasy made up by Kim to get others to do terrible things for her."

With so many people aware of the true, malicious nature of Snibson, it is baffling how few people voiced their concerns to law enforcement. Snibson continued her search for willing participants until she found two men who believed her lies. Her first recruit was Andrew Flentjar. He was a neighbor of the Snibson family, although Mr Snibson insists that he didn't know Flentjar that well, and had believed that Snibson hadn't either.

"She didn't socialize with (him) or stay for a cuppa," he had said in an interview. But still Snibson had managed to make the otherwise reasonable man willing to help her in her plan to kidnap and assault Mr Hosa.

"Andrew was told by Kim that the couple had sexually abused her child and had videoed the episode," Paul Leask, a Crown Prosecutor for New South Wales, reviled on the television show Deadly Women.

In her interview on the same television show, a journalist for Illawarra Mercury Newspaper, Veronica Apap, attested that there had been "no evidence at any time in court that Kathryn or Greg had engaged in anything like that." Still, Flintjar believed the story Snibson wove and, under the impression that her plan only involved minor assault as justice for her daughter, agreed to help.

Snibson then approached Stacy Lea-Caton, a former neighbor who had been in trouble with the law. Mr Snibson remembers Lea-Caton as being a man who continuously worked to create a notable reputation for himself as a dangerous man.

"You would be talking about normal things," Mr Snibson told Ms Apap during an interview, "and Stacey would come in with something bigger or better. He talked about his criminal history, stuff like that."

Mr Snibson went on to say that when it came to Mr Lea-Caton he "didn't believe anything he told me", and that, "I didn't think he would go very well in a fight, myself. He is not this tough person he was making himself out to be."

Ms Snibson, however, saw a potential for violence in Lea-Caton and knew just how to bring it to the surface. During a visit she tested the waters by telling him a lie similar to the one she had recruited Flintjar with. According to Leask, "Stacey Lea-Caton was told by her that the couple had drugged her, sexually assaulted her, and videoed the episode."

Once again there she could produce any evidence in support of her claims, nor could later investigators. According to Apap, "It seems to be a total fantasy on her part" and Mr Snibson has stated that "Greg Hosa was a thoroughly decent person who did not deserve such terrible lies to be made up about him, let alone die so needlessly." Still, Snibson was convincing enough to for Lea-Coton to push aside his desire to get his life back on track and he soon found himself alongside Flintjar, embroiled in Snibson's supposed plan for vigilante justice.

"She employed a means of modulating the story depending on the person who was the recipient of it. To press the right buttons." Leask asserted. "The theme was always one of sexual impropriety and of course, nothing excites people's sympathy more than that."

With her two accomplices waiting for instructions, Snibson put her plan into action on January 28th, 2006. It was easy to lure Hosa to her home. The 56-year-old man didn't suspect that anything might be wrong when Snibson called and asked him to come over.

"He came quickly after that conversation occurred," Apap said in her Deadly Women interview. "He didn't think that he was in any danger or that there would be any problem."

Lea-Carton and Flintjar swarmed Hosa as he entered the Snibson home. Using a slab of wood they struck him on the head and forced him to the ground. The men then proceeded to hogtie Hosa, forcing him onto his stomach and binding his legs to his hands. It was during this attack that Hosa asked his assailants "why is this happening?" While the exact wording cannot be determined, it is reported that Flintjar responded by accusing Hosa of pedophilia.

With this declaration both of Snibson's henchmen realized that they had been lied to. They were blindsided by the revelation yet, having participated in assault and kidnapping, and still unaware of just how malicious Snibson's intentions were, neither felt they were in a position to leave. Snibson deceit had taken them past the point of no return and both were at a loss at what to do next. This afforded Snibson the perfect environment to maintain control.

While the men watched over a struggling Hosa, Snibson called his wife and 'confessed' that she and Hosa had been having an affair. It was a story that few would believe and later would be seen by their family as adding a foul insult to considerable injury. Jan Keily, a sister of McKay, would attest that they family was 'disgusted' by the claim. But on that night, it was enough to draw McKay into Snibon's trap.

Just like her husband, 44-year-old McKay was set upon by Lea-Carton and Flintjar. She too was hogtied and gagged by having a sock forced into her mouth and taped into place. Once again the men found themselves forced into a situation far from what they had been expecting when Snibson left to retrieve two 44-gallon drums from Champagne Shires and brought them to the house.

After shoving Ms McKay into one of the drums Snibson disclosed the needlessly cruel method she had chosen in order to kill McKay. "She murdered Kathryn by wrapping tape around her face and eyes and nose," Leask described.

Many factors must be considered when determining how long it would take an individual to suffocate to death. First, oxygen deprivation renders the victim unconscious. If they are still unable to breath brain damage will begin. As a general guide, it is believed to take approximately 5-6 minutes for death to occur. Snibson, Lea-Carton, and Flintjar stood by and watched McKay struggle for this entire length of time. When arrested, all three would give varying statements as to what exactly had happened that night, but in all versions, the two men who had not agreed to murder still made no attempt to save Ms McKay.

When Snibson turned her attention back to Hosa, she had a different method in mind for his execution. According to Leask, "Kim killed Greg Hosa by garrotting him with electrical wire. Kim killed them both deliberately and methodically." And once again, her now reluctant accomplices failed to put an end to her actions.

As night fell the trio loaded the two barrels, each now filled with the corpses of a once loving couple, into the back of Snibson's truck. Together the three drove to a remote patch of the Tomerong State Forest. Here she doused the remains of Ms McKay and Mr Hosa with petrol and set them alight.

As Leask stated, "Incinerating the bodies was done for no other purpose than to destroy evidence that those two poor people had ever been to Kim's house that day."

For all her obsession and manipulation, it took only hours for Snibson's plan to come undone. As it would turn out, Mr Snibson's reading of Stacey Lea-Caton's character had been far more reliable that Kim's had been. The only known criminal within the trio, Lea-Carton was unable to suppress his guilty conscious and within hours of leaving Snibson confessed to his sister and her husband. The series of events he told them had been highly edited but it was still damning enough that the young couple had insisted that he tell the authorities. At 2:30am they had taken him to the Nowra Police Station to report the crime. According to police, Lea-Caton had originally stated that he had seen a man and woman tried up at the farm and was worried that they might come to harm. By 8:00am they had arrested Snibson. A whole day hadn't passed by the time police located the remains of Greg Hosa and Kathryn McKay. Superintendent Kyle Stewart would describe the discovery as a "horrific scene", while Leask provided greater detail. "All that remained of Kathryn was her right foot and little remained of Greg."

But even when caught Snibson was far from willing to admit to her actions. In her statements to the police, she was a hapless witness to a domestic disturbance that spiraled out of control. According to Snibson, she had informed Ms McKay that she had been having an affair with Mr Hosa. Hosa had come to her home first, followed by and enraged Ms McKay. Once there, the couple had begun to argue. The confrontation soon grew volatile and in the heat of the moment

Lea-Caton had picked up a bird perch and struck Mr Hose over the head hard enough that he fell to the ground. She recounted how this hadn't deterred Ms McKay who had then turned her anger onto Snibson herself. McKay had become so furious that she had 'come at' Snibson. This had forced Flentjar, who had also happened to be present, to tackle the older woman to keep her from harming Snibson.

"She fell back and hit her head on the pantry and fell on the floor," Snibson told police. She further went on to explain that is was after Ms McKay had been injured that Lea-Caton's murderous intent rose to the surface. In Snibson's version of events, it was Lea-Caton that strangled Hosa with a rope before forcing her to wrap tape around McKay's head until, as she insisted he had instructed, 'she turned blue'. In his final act of depravity, Lea-Caton had been the one to light the bodies on fire.

Her behavior at the trials of her accomplices was a far cry from what others had observed during her own trial. While giving evidence in the New South Wales Supreme Court, Snibson broke down into tears as she described the "gurgling sounds" Mr Hosa made as the life was choked out of him. Snibson would tell the court that she felt "sick to my stomach" about the murders. She continued to say that she thought about it "every single day." She had become so unsettled that Justice Terence Buddin had to adjourn the sentencing hearing for five minutes to give her time to compose herself.

Compared to her behavior and demeanor at other times it was almost possible to believe Ms Snibson was two entirely different people. For Leask, there was no doubt which persona was ligament and which she put on for self-preservation.

"There will be no remorse from Kim Snibson. It's not in her nature," he had said in an interview. He also claimed that Snibson is a person "that lacks the quality that makes us human beings." But perhaps his opinion on Snibson was most elegantly and directly described within his statement, "I have been involved in some shocking crimes involving some dreadful brutality. This case stands out because, in my career, I can only reasonably expect to come across one or two sociopaths. And that's what Kim Snibson is."

It is a sentiment echoed by Candice DeLong, a former criminal profiler for the Federal Bureau of Investigation who often lends her insights to programs such as Deadly Women. "It's unlikely Kim feels remorse for what she did. Sociopaths never do," she said during an interview. She further asserted that "if she ever does emerge from prison, watch out."

It is DeLong's opinion that "Kim is a natural born killer. She wanted to commit murder," but for those like her ex-husband, Snibson is not so clearly an evil woman. While he called her 'pure evil' in an interview with Take-5 Magazine it was also discovered that he had withheld information from investigators in a bid to protect her from prosecution.

"I did tell the truth in all statements," he told the New South Wales Supreme Court. "I left out those couple of sentences from Kim because it sounded very damning to me. I didn't want to see anything bad happen to her. I still had loyalty to Kim even though we had long broken up."

Some of these omitted sentences referred to statements Ms Snibson had made the day after her arrest. According to Mr Snibson, she had said "Don't worry about me, I'm a bad person", and had alluded that she would be 'going away' for 30 years. He further stated that Snibson had said that while she did want to tell him what had happened on the night of the murders her lawyer had instructed her not to talk about it. "She said when she gets to court and has her say, the truth will come out."

Whether Mr Snibson truly believes in his ex-wife's innocence or not, he unwittingly brought more evidence against her. When Detective Sergeant Jason Hogan had asked Mr Snibson to take them to where he as Ms Snibson used to train their dogs for dog sled competitions he had agreed. The location he had led them to had been the where the smoldering barrels holding the remains of McKay and Hosa had been found. In the same day, he had also unknowingly brought the police to the part of Braidwood Road where Mr Hosa's burnt out four-wheel drive had been discovered.

Andrew Wayne Flentjar was the first to be sentenced. He is currently serving a minimum of 10-years for his role in assisting in the kidnapping of Hosa and McKay. Stacey Lea-Caton pleaded guilty to aiding and abetting murder and received a sentence of a minimum 16 years, with the maximum time served of 22-years.

Lea-Caton testified against Snibson during her trail and put a great amount of pressure on her supposed version of events. Combined with the sight of the 44-gallon drums, similar to those used to dispose of McKay and Hosa's remains, which were brought into the courtroom, the cracks in Snibson's account of that night were beginning to show. Whatever the 10 men and 2 women of the jury had truly believed was rendered moot when, approximately halfway through her trial, Snibson changed her plea to guilty.

On September 5th, 2008 Snibson faced her sentencing hearing. By Australian law, those affected by a crime have the right to lodge and read out a victim impact statement to the court and the perpetrator. The friends and family of Hosa and McKay took advantage of this opportunity. Marion, Katheryn McKay's sister, described how the murders had rendered her family into a state similar to 'animals caught in headlights'. In her statement, she explained how she struggled "to find the words for the numbness and traumatic feelings the murders caused the family."

Marion described the impact of their loss and Snibson's actions as being felt "physically, socially, emotionally and psychologically." How her family is no longer able to watch programs about horses or the news, as they stir up too many painful memories. How her work as a counselor has suffered and that the majority of her grief-stricken family has since abandoned their homes in Nowra.

She described McKay and Hosa as loving, community-minded people, and reminded the court and Snibson that her sister had been a nurse with a natural drive and desire to help other people. She reiterated how their senseless and brutal deaths have had a lasting impact on hundreds of other people and how more than 500 people had attended their funerals. Somewhere within this speech, Kim Snibson reportedly began to cry.

Another of McKay's sisters, Jan Keily, spoke of her utter confusion at how Snibson, Flintjar, and Lea-Caton could have brought themselves to do what they had done. She also addressed how insulting it was to the memories or their loved ones that Snibson still maintained that there had been an affair, not to mention the accusations she had made about McKay's intended violence towards Snibson. "The families are shocked by the lies that have been told about Kathryn McKay and Gregory Hosa by the three offenders."

Justice Buddin commended the sisters for the dignity and grace they had shown while delivering their statements before adjourning the proceedings. When he delivered the final verdict, Justice Buddin gave his own opinion on the case before him. He expressed how the crimes against this kind-hearted couple had been committed with a "considerable degree of callousness".

Justice Buddin explored the suffering that was inflicted upon Mr Hosa and Ms McKay, not just at the agonizingly slow and painful death, but at the mental torture that must have endured at the hands of the captors. He expressed how they were forced to wait for a "not inconsiderable amount of time", stuck in a state of anguish, wondering what their kidnappers would decide to do to them. "They were totally defenseless and at the mercy of the offenders," he said.

Justice Buddin then turned his attention to the version of events that Snibson had put forth, the version of events that left her as a victim of circumstances and Lea-Coton's vicious nature. He described this story as "implausible", "quite fanciful" and "tailored to suit inescapable, objective facts". As proof of the ridiculousness of her claims, he pointed to her recruitment of accomplices. This was not an act of a woman caught off guard by a lover's spat but instead was indicative of the level of calculation and manipulation she was capable of wilfully wielding.

While Snibson had told the court that she was sorry for the role she had played in the couple's grizzly end, Justice Buddin was not swayed. He explained that he had not believed her words to be those of someone truly remorseful and repentant, but instead said that whatever contrition she had expressed struck him as contrived. His final verdict had been a jail sentence of no less than 32 years. This means that Snibson would be 60-years-old before she becomes eligible to apply for parole.

The town of Nowra is still healing from the horrors of that singular night. As Paul Leask has stated, "that one of their own was the killer was something that psychologically traumatized that community." The senseless cruelty Snibson brought down upon a devoted, generous couple has only been magnified by the ridiculousness of her plan. For all the action she was willing to take there was no way her plan would allow her to gain ownership of Champagne Shire, rendering her depraved actions useless and her goal unattainable.

But perhaps what is hardest for the residents of Nowra, and all that hear of the tragic deaths of McKay and Hosa, to come to terms with, is the wealth of opportunities presented for people to intervene. Be it out of embarrassment or social delicacy, those who had concerns over Sibson's actions had refused to disclose what they had known. At the time it might have been dismissed as a personal eccentricity, a misunderstanding, or a benign threat, but now blaze as warning signs for the brutality that was to come. Perhaps if those who had felt the inkling of concern had stepped forward a different course could have been plotted and McKay and Hosa could have been spared. But then it is also possible that nothing could have deterred Snibson, and that these murders were the only end her insatiable greed would have allowed. Wherever the truth may lie, it is too late to act for McKay and Hosa. Their lives have already been sacrificed on the altar of Snibson's pride. The only solace that is to be garnished now is that Snibson has been removed from the general population and will hopefully be unable to claim any further victims. But what little comfort this offers will forever be overshadowed by the influence Snibon's name will forever provoke. Those who learn about the merciless crimes this woman visited upon the people who would have been her friends will undoubtedly no longer be able to look at their neighbors without there being the lingering question of 'what if?'

SHE KILLED THE PREACHER

John Fontaine

55

The Case of Mary Winkler

Mary Winkler, at first appearances, would seem to be an altogether normal woman. So too did her family, with a husband who was a Church minister and three young children, girls aged just eight, six and one.

The family lived in Selmer, Tenn., a small town occupied by around 4,500 people, according to the 2015 census. The town is situated to the south west of the state. Not much has happened in Selmer; the most famous person to have been born there was Chad Harville, former pitcher for the Oakland A's, and for one year, the Red Sox. He achieved a 4-9 win-loss record over his career in the MLB.

Today, the most famous- or infamous- person to have come from Selmer is Mary Winkler. In 2006, Mary sparked a border-crossing manhunt, and a court case followed nationwide. She had killed her husband with a shot to the back from the family's shotgun. But it was the gripping, and at times bizarre, court case which gripped the attention of the nation.

Matthew dead, Mary and the family Missing

The date was March 6th, 2007. It was a Tuesday like any other. Mary and Matthew were at home all day together, although Matthew was due to give a sermon that evening.

It was actually members of Matthew's congregation who found his body that night. They had visited his home to check up on him after he had missed the service he was set to give; instead, they found him lying dead, having been shot in the back.

There was no sign of Mary or any of their children at the home, and as such, they were reported missing. The authorities quickly sent out an Amber Alert, since nobody had any idea what could have happened to them, or where they might be. Family and friends had no information to provide police on their whereabouts.

There was every chance that the family had been kidnapped or murdered, and their bodies disposed of elsewhere, although police could not identify a break in, and had no reason to believe that anything of value had been stolen.

It was only a day later that she was arrested in Alabama, having run from the family home with her young children. They were found 350 miles away from home, at Orange Beach, and in the back seat of the van was the family's shotgun. It was certainly suspicious; but what reason could Mary have possibly had for committing such a crime?

The Trial

In the build up to the case going to trial, public interest ramped up. Speculation had been rife about why Mary would have murdered her husband, a seemingly nice, well respected member of the local community. Perhaps either one of them had had an affair, and Matthew had been killed in a crime of passion. Or maybe he had been killed for an insurance claim?

As such, the press reported every step of the story as it came out during the hearing. The trial began when a Tennessee Bureau of Investigation Agent John Mehr read a statement that Mary had made very soon after her arrest. In it, Mary claimed that the couple had been arguing about their family finances, before Mary had shot her husband with their 12 gauge shotgun. She had said that the last thing she had wanted was to actually murder her husband, but she had been brandishing the gun in an effort to convince him to work through their problems, together. The argument had been ongoing throughout the day, and Mary had finally snapped, resorting to drastic measures to be able to convince him. She had never intended to kill him: she had said in the statement, 'I don't want this at all. I don't want any of this to be, at all.'

The statement continued on, and Mary claimed that they had argued often and argued fiercely. 'He had really been on me lately,' Mary had said, 'criticizing me for things- the way I walk, I eat, everything. It was just building up to a point. I was tired of it. I guess I got to a point and snapped.'

At first glance, it would seem that Mary had simply lost her composure, become angry, and killed her husband 'as the red mist had descended'. But after their initial statement, Mary's attorney indicated that there was much more that would come out about Matthew's behaviour when she testified which would help to explain her actions. Clearly, there were more problems with their marriage than the occasional, albeit fierce, argument.

Mary's Crime

The case for the prosecution wasted no time in painting Mary as a cold blooded killer, who left her husband to die without remorse. Admittedly, the plain facts of the case made Mary seem unbelievably guilty. The prosecution relied on several of these facts in their attempt to convince the jury of Mary's guilt for the charge of murder.

Mary had disconnected the phone immediately after she shot her husband, stopping him from being able to call the emergency services, or receive any calls that may have come in. This suggested that Mary had been in full control of her actions, not panicking, since it is unlikely that somebody in a state of anxiety would think to disconnect the phone.

The fact that Mary had attempted to flee to Orange Beach, Alabama, was also a key point for the prosecution. Immediately after Matthew's death, Mary had taken the family minivan to the beach, with her three children. Later on in her defence, Mary would claim that she ran because '[n]obody would believe me, and they'd take the girls away and put me away.' Certainly, in many murder cases, the fact that the defendant flees the scene is a certain indicator of guilt.

The family's daughter Patricia testified that she couldn't understand her mother's actions. All that she knew was that she had heard a 'big boom', and the sound of something heavy hitting the floor. She quickly ran to the bedroom to see her father on the floor, and her mother holding the shotgun. She had no idea what could possibly have provoked her mother to shoot him.

Another sticking point was that the family finances had been 'in shambles' just before the murder had taken place. This had led Mary to become embroiled in what is called a 'check kiting' scam. In it, she had received checks from unidentified accounts in Canada and Nigeria, and had ultimately fallen to a financial scam that had lost the family money. Prosecutors claimed that this could have somehow instigated the argument that led to Matthew's death, and that Mary had felt as if she had no way out of the scam.

They also jumped on the fact that in an initial conversation with investigators, Mary had told them that their marriage was a happy one, and that '[t]here's no poor me. I'm in control.' They clearly wanted to paint a picture of Mary as remorseless, deceitful, and smarter than she looked.

The Cross-examination

During her cross-examination in court, Mary stated that she didn't remember grabbing the gun from the closet in which it was kept. What she did remember was that 'something went off', 'hearing a loud boom', and that 'it wasn't as loud as I thought it would be.' She did admit that she had shot her husband. Matthew rolled from the bed- upon which he had been lying as they had argued- and dropped to the floor. Mary described smelling gunpowder.

Prosecutor Walter Freeland asked her whether she understood that 'pulling a trigger is what makes it go boom', to which she replied that she did.

Matthew asked her why she had snapped and shot him. She could only say 'I'm sorry.' The shotgun blast had been inflicted from behind, directly into Matthew's back, and had caused severe damage to his organs and spine. According to prosecutors, he had in fact still been alive as Mary had run from the house.

But these simple facts were far from the end of the story, as Mary was to reveal.

Appearances and Revelations

At first, Mary spoke of her husband not in the past tense, but in the present, as if she couldn't quite understand how final her actions really had been. In reminiscing about happier times, Mary told the court that her husband was an intelligent, social man, and that the family had shared many 'good times' together. She also seemed to enjoy talking about her children, and the happiness they brought her.

This happy family life, however, was simply one side of the marriage. Mary's attorney stated that '[w]hat went on behind their closed doors is going to have to be told ... Some of what we've got from the state of Tennessee touches on sexual abuse.' Their defence was that Matthew had made Mary's life a 'living hell': '[w]e will show you proof that he would destroy objects that she loved, he would isolate her from her family and he would abuse her not just verbally, not just emotional and not just physically—in other ways, too.'

Just before the murder, Mary claimed that Matthew had been threatening their children and even attempted to throttle their infant daughter, Breanna. He had been shouting, angry, because he had wanted a son. As the case went on, it became obvious that this was only the tip of the iceberg, however, and more and more sordid details of their home life would come to light.

Matthew, Mary claimed, was a violent, abusive husband. Shortly after their marriage, he ordered her to stop socialising with any of her family and friends (a common tactic among abusive spouses in order to further isolate their partners from potential help). Winkler's sisters described how Mary seemed stuck in her marriage, unhappy, but unable to leave. In an interview, they said that 'As the years went on, she seemed to be nervous to show love towards us.'

Mary was commonly 'screamed and hollered' at by her husband. 'He just flailed. He's a big guy and he was just all over ... He'd point his finger inches away from my nose. Whatever he was upset about, it was my fault,' Mary had said. It could be over anything: 'I was fat, my hair wasn't right, the girls, if something went wrong, it was my fault. I didn't know when it was coming.' Mary described her situation as one familiar to abused wives and husbands across America.

Her attorney, Steve Farese, provided further information based on his conversations with Mary. She had needed her husband's permission for everything, even for getting her hair cut. 'This was constant, and she lived a life where she walked on eggshells.' This abuse, he said, had given Mary symptoms of post traumatic stress disorder, simply because 'she didn't know what was going to happen next.' Furthermore, a psychologist testified as part of Mary's defence, saying that her symptoms were those of clinical depression and PTSD.

During her time on the stand, Mary also claimed that Matthew had forced her to watch pornography with him, and that he had bought her several 'slutty' costumes for sex, which she normally would never have worn, but for fear of her husband. If she refused, Matthew wouldn't hesitate to get physical, hitting her or even using his belt to whip her. Mary famously produced a wig and a pair of white high heels in the witness box during her cross-examination to show the court evidence of Matthew's other side.

Mary stated that she was never happy watching pornography, dressing up in sexy outfits or performing the sex acts that Matthew wanted. She went along with his ideas, however, because she didn't dare face his reaction if she didn't. 'I'd just do anything to help him stay happy.' Throughout these revelations, Mary was visibly embarrassed and uncomfortable. Clearly she would have preferred that none of them had ever come to light; but Mary felt it necessary to brave what her neighbors, and the nation, might think in order to clear her name and justify her actions.

Mary's family had been quick to corroborate her side of the story. Her father, Clark Freeman, had spoken out through Good Morning America and detailed the 'physical, mental, verbal' abuse that his daughter had suffered. Other friends came forward during the court case, and gave similar verdicts on their relationship. A friend of Mary's,

Rudie Thomsen, said that '[o]ne Sunday, Mary came into the church and I looked at her and she had a black eye.' Similarly, Mary's friend Amy Redmon agreed that Matthew had been controlling: '[h]e was an authority figure, and he made the decisions basically. It was obvious.'

Conversely, Matthew's family denied that their son had been anything like Mary had depicted in her defence testimony. Matthew's father, Charles Daniel Winkler, said that his son was a kind, gentle man, who could have done nothing to justify what the defence was claiming. Diane spoke several times during the trial, lashing out at Mary: 'You've never told your girls you're sorry! Don't you think you at least owe them that?'

The dramatic story of a supposedly kindly, gentle church minister having such a sordid, cruel and abusive hidden life gripped America. The case was covered extensively on all major networks, discussed on late night panel shows

The Jury's Verdict

While the prosecutors had tried to convince the jury to convict her on a charge of first degree murder, they were unsuccessful. The jury came to their verdict by April, that year. It took them eight hours to deliberate their way to the decision; this mirrored the response of the nation, which was similarly undecided on just what punishment Mary really deserved.

Mary was found guilty of voluntary manslaughter, a charge which carries a far more lenient sentence than murder. While murderers can receive full life sentences, and in certain states receive the death penalty, the maximum sentence for voluntary manslaughter is only 6 years.

Mary showed little emotion at the verdict, but did embrace each of her relatives afterwards. In a show of support, her family had been sat in the row behind her, and all linked arms with one another to demonstrate their solidarity. Afterwards, she was taken back into custody to await sentencing.

Mary's attorney stated afterwards that Mary's testimony had been central in securing the more lenient sentence. 'I think Mary's testimony was integral in this decision. They had to hear it from Mary', Farese told the press. 'They judged her credibility and they saw that she had an abusive relationship and they made their judgment based upon that.'

For Mary, the most important implication of the verdict was that she could finally begin to think of being reunited with her children. Speaking on her behalf after the trial, Farese continued: 'We would like to do so many things to open up communication between Mary and the paternal grandparents and to get the children out of this cycle of constant upheaval over this terrible tragic event.' But the question of how long she would be in prison remained.

Mary's sentencing was scheduled for May 18th, at which point both Mary and the prosecution would have a final chance to address the court before the judge decided on the final jail term. However, the situation looked positive for Mary. Not only would the five months that she had been imprisoned awaiting trial be taken into consideration, but the judge had indicated that alternatives to incarceration would be on the table. Perhaps Mary could avoid jail time altogether.

Sentencing: The Trial at an End

Due to a scheduling error, the hearing took place around three weeks late, on June 8th.

Mary took to the stand one last time to plead for mercy. She read aloud from a prepared statement, telling Matthew's family of her sorrow and remorse for her actions. She was 'so sorry that this had happened', and would 'always miss and love' her husband. 'I ask for mercy and understanding, but I know whatever decision you reach today will be right ... I ask you to please let me go home today and be with my children.' Tabitha Freeman- Mary's sister- had also pleaded for leniency, in particular to let Mary be reunited with her children. She went as far as calling Mary 'the best example of a good person I can think of'.

Members of Matthew's family, too, took to the stand to plead their case for the prosecution. Charles and his wife were clearly hurt and in disbelief at Mary's actions both in murdering their son, and believed that Mary had purposefully smeared his name at trial. 'The monster that you have painted for the world to see? I don't think that monster existed,' Diane Winkler had said.

After speaking their pieces, all that Mary, her family, and Matthew's parents could do was wait until the judge's decision. The trial- as well as the very public 'trial' that Mary had been through in the media- was finally at an end.

The defence had requested that Mary be granted full probation, or judicial diversion, both outcomes which would have meant that Mary would spent no further time in prison, and even that her record would be cleared of wrongdoing altogether. This request was denied.

After recess, Mary was told that she would spend 3 years in prison for her crime. But Circuit Judge J. Weber McCraw reduced that amount to just 210 days total in prison before she would be allowed to leave on probation. She also had that sentence reduced further, due to the fact that she had spent five months incarcerated waiting for trial.

Moreover, that time would be spent not in jail, but in a mental health centre in Tennessee. There, she would receive treatment for both her depression and post traumatic stress disorder. After such a long ordeal, with the prosecution fighting to either put Mary on death row or to imprison her indefinitely, it seemed that she had gotten off with hardly a slap on the wrist.

Steve Farese branded the sentence 'a victory': '[s]he could be in prison for life, and that's what everybody thought she was headed for to begin with.' Her other attorney, Leslie Ballin, said '[s]he'll be able to get out and fight the battle she wants to, and that is to get her children back.' Mary could finally think about the future again.

But certain signs indicated that it would not be as easy to reconcile with her children and family as she might hope. Matthew's family left the courtroom without making a comment to the press, as did the prosecution, clearly disappointed in the verdict. They gave no indication that they would be happy to open dialogue about Mary's daughters- not with the woman whom they believed to have murdered their son in cold blood.

The aftermath of Mary's release

Mary was released on August 14th, 2007. She had only been sentenced the previous June.

Upon her release, her lawyer informed the press that Mary would not be speaking with them, to maintain her privacy. During her time in the mental health facility, Mary could finally begin her attempt to win full custody of her three daughters, and she was still fighting this case at the time of her release. She had not seen her children, apart from Patricia's brief testimony as part of the case, for over a year. Throughout the case, and after Mary's release, her children were staying with Matthew's family.

Moreover, she was still fighting a $2 million dollar civil lawsuit filed by Matthew's parents. They also took legal measures, which, if successful, would have meant that the custody of Mary's children remained with them.

After her release, Mary seemed happier to her family and friends. From an outside perspective, it could be easy to claim that this was just as much due to her happiness at avoiding a jail sentence as it was to her being rid of an abuser. She was in fact living with friends at first after her release, and went back to work at a dry cleaners in McMinnville, Tenn., 200 miles from Selmer.

In the same interview as was mentioned before, Mary's sisters agreed that she had changed entirely. After years of shyness, Mary seeming unable or unwilling to show love to them for fear of her husband's violence, she seemed to finally be able to open up. 'Now it's back to the old Mary [who] loves us and doesn't care to come and hug us and gives us a kiss on the cheek.'

Since then, Mary lived in McMinnville. She has moved between jobs, working at the dry cleaners, before starting work at a nursery. She briefly dated the brother of one of her most vocal supporters, Paul Pillow; afterwards, she moved in with Wayne Cantrell, a preacher living in Smithville nearby.

Mary regained custody of her three children in 2008, but by 2010, received the news that she had multiple sclerosis. Her diagnosis came at the worst time, as she was settling down in her new life; she had not long started medical school with the desire to become a nurse, and had to quit since the work would be too demanding. She hasn't returned to work since.

One comfort for Mary was that Matthew's parents seemed close to being able to forgive her. After her diagnosis, they gave Mary some time off from parenting by taking care of the children for a weekend, which soon turned into several months. Daniel Winkler has preached several times since the events on the topic of forgiveness, although when asked by local press why he chose the topic, he has refused to answer, presumably preferring to keep those details private.

Mary, too, preferred to put the past behind her. In an interview with WAFF 48, the NBC affiliate in Huntsville AL., she stated how she would prefer to stay out of the limelight, particularly for the sake of her girls. 'Whatever reason people have any problem with me, that's fine. Everybody's entitled to their opinion, but these girls are treated for who they are, not because of what their mother's done ... They're three very fine young ladies'.

Concluding Thoughts

Some members of the public reacted with disgust at the abnormally short sentence that Mary was given, and questioned whether a husband would have been given the same leniency as Mary was. Men's rights activist Glenn Sacks publicly questioned whether a man would have been shown such leniency, and pointed to the case of Scott Peterson (who received the death penalty for the murder of his pregnant wife) to indicate that no, a man would not. He also argued that the idea of abuse had been widened to include simple criticism, and should therefore not necessarily be used as defence of murder.

Conversely, there have been many women put in prison for murdering their abusive husbands, some for much longer than Mary Winkler. The 'battered woman defense', or the preferred terminology today of 'battering and its effects', is not a genuine legal defence in itself; it can, however, be used to convince a court of diminished responsibility. Its effectiveness is due to the sympathy that it elicits from jurors, who can be convinced that abuse is a form of provocation, and the murder a form of self defense. Under this defense, Mary's short sentence makes sense.

The case has remained a touch stone with regards to spousal abuse in the U.S. A made-for-TV movie, 'The Pastor's Wife', was released in 2011. It was based on the book of the same title, written by Dianne Fanning, an award winning crime writer. The story was changed somewhat, with the inclusion of a financial subplot involving tax fraud. However, it also made use of real life interviews with people who knew the Winklers- including Matthew's parents. His mother revealed that she could never believe Mary's story. Charles admitted that Mary's story could be true, and that he could forgive her if she confessed her purposeful intention to murder Matthew.

As for the community in which the family had lived, the reaction was largely one of forgiveness. According to members of that community, the town's 'Christian roots and ... its tendency to give people the benefit of the doubt' meant that they took Mary at her word. Mary's quite life in McMinnville and Smithville similarly shows that the American public would rather leave her and her family alone after their painful ordeal.

TRACEY, TRACEY

Greg Symons

Claiming to be a victim of rape and other abuses, a distraught Tracey Grissom would travel to her ex-husband Hunter's workplace and shoot him six times in the back, receiving a twenty-five-year life sentence for his murder.

Her defense attorney would argue that Tracey was motivated by post-traumatic stress disorder caused by her Hunter's constant abuse and sexual assaults. One jury member had even asked the judge to be lenient in her sentencing as they were not allowed to hear details of her Hunter's alleged abuses (beatings, rape, sodomy).

But what really happened in the years that led up to May 15th, 2012? Was she in fact the victim of years of abuse by a psychotic husband? Or did she want to cash in on his $100,000 life insurance policy?

INSTANT ATTRACTION

The couple would meet during a dinner party in 2003 in Tuscaloosa, Alabama. Tracey was twenty-one years old and going through a divorce. She had a son, James Michael, from the previous marriage.

Family and friends would describe the union as "love at first sight." Hunter was blown away by the young Tracey's blue eyes and facial beauty.

"For him, it was love at first sight," crime author William Phelps said. "She was gorgeous."

A whirlwind courtship would ensue and the couple would elope in 2004.

"In the beginning, it was good," Tracey told CBS' 48 hours. "We had a friendship. Just your normal, honeymoon phase marriage."

"He was fun," Tracey said. "And he was attractive."

Hunter was two years younger than Tracey, however, and his mother felt that he had jumped the gun too early in the relationship.

Her words proved to be prophetic as after only eight months into the marriage, the marriage went south.

According to Tracey, their marital problems began with Hunter's drug addiction.

"I had caught him smoking marijuana," Tracey said. "Doing illegal things could cause a problem and I couldn't risk losing my son over."

Tracey claimed that she threatened her new spouse with a divorce but Hunter gave her his word that he would stop with his drug use. She stated that the relationship improved and the decided to start a construction company together.

"I took out an equity line to start a company," Tracey said. "Which was Grissom Construction. It was all in my name."

Hunter specialized in building elaborate boat docks. He had an artistic eye and could do docks, stairs, and other accouterments. The business began to grow in short order.

"They're going to take on the world," Phelps said. "They're going to be entrepreneurs and they're gonna make it."

They then had a daughter of their own, Anna Grace. The child was a long time coming for the couple. They had been trying for a long time as Tracey had five miscarriages before Anna Grace was born.

"She was premature," Tracey recalled. "Her heart and lungs were not developed. A very stressful time."

Behind closed doors things were rocky. On the surface, however, things looked good. They had a young family and were making money.

"All-American family," Phelps said. "White-picket fence. The whole nine yards. Middle-class. Suburbia. Maybe the Prince Charming that she's been waiting for."

But again, this was only on the surface. Tracey harbored secrets of her own. One of which was her own addiction to prescription drugs.

"Psychologically, there's something going on here," Phelps said. "There's something going on behind those beautiful eyes and it ain't good."

Tracey would often turn on on the children, showing off her temper. Then she would turn on Hunter.

"This would cause friction in the marriage," Phelps said. "And where there's friction, there's fire."

SETTING THE STAGE

Tracey would later state that Hunter would "act strangely" shortly before she filed divorce. She was a registered nurse and gave him an over-the-counter drug test. According to her, Hunter tested posted for marijuana, Oxycontin, opiates, and methamphetamine.

Hunter would later be arrested for marijuana possession but his family would insist that he never did the harder drugs.

Tracey would file for divorce in the summer of 2010 after six years of marriage. According to her, this would prompt physical abuse from Hunter.

Hunter had to move out but their divorce agreement would allow him access to the home.

"In September of 2010," Tracey recalled. "That was the first time he physically hit me. It (the abuse) got progressively worse. He had made the comments that if I told anybody he would kill me. I believed him."

Hunter' co-workers and family members would have a different take on the situation, however. His co-workers remembered a time when she tracked him down at one of the jobs and made a scene.

"She's screaming, jumping on him," Hunter's co-worker said. "Said something about him having another girlfriend and used the expression about, 'You are mine. I'll kill you. I'll kill you. You are mine."

"She's borderline demonic," Hunter's mother said. " mean, I absolutely believe—that she is that troubled."

Hunter's family continued to believe that he did not abuse Tracey.

"He did not have an abusive, an angry bone in his body," Hunter's aunt Gina said. "In fact, we kind of laughed at him because he was too laid-back."

The divorce was finalized in October of 2010.

EVIDENCE OF ABUSE?

Loran Richards was the first of Tracey's friends to notice the minor injuries on her body. She would inquire about the bruises but the answers she received were always evasive. Seeing Tracey with a black eye, however, forced her to try and get more answers.

"I said, Tracey, you may have terrible luck," Richards recalled. "But nobody is so unlucky that they trip, fall down the stairs, and hit their face on a baseball in the eye socket. So don't give me a lame excuse. You don't have to give me any excuse, but let's take a picture."

Tracey broke down. She gave her friend all of the grisly details, detailing the abuse she suffered at the hands of Hunter. Loran then became her advocate, taking pictures of Tracey's injuries. She would later state that she saw blood stains and other signs of abuse at Tracey's home.

THAT FATEFUL NIGHT

Now divorced, Hunter would arrive at Tracey's home on November 22nd, 2010.

According to Tracey, he then became enraged when Tracey told him that she had spent the night with a new lover.

"He told me that he was gonna kill me," Tracey recalled. Tracey stated that she tried to escape, running into the closet in order to "get away from the kids and to pray." Tracey's eleven-year-old son from a previous relationship was in the home as was the four-year-old daughter they have together.

Hunter caught up with her and knocked her to the ground. He tied a belt around her ankles and then began choking her.

Half-conscious, Tracey alleged to have been raped and sodomized.

The brutal attack would leave Tracey unconscious. She would wake up the next morning on the bathroom floor.

"I called Hunter," Tracey recalled. "I told him that I was bleeding and that I was hurt and that I needed help. And he told me, 'Fuck you. I hope you die.'"

Tracey wound up in the emergency room after the attack. Hospital records would show that she had a laceration on her head, bruises, and ligature marks on her feet.

Tracey would then be referred to the Turning Point domestic violence center.

Marian Waters would describe Tracey's injuries as among the worst she had ever seen in a twenty-year career.

Waters would testify that Tracey had suffered a horrific assault. She described her mental state as typical of someone who had just been raped; fearful, jumpy, fearing for her life.

Tracey had suffered a hematoma on her side that was the side of a grapefruit. She also claimed to have experienced rectal nerve damage which would require surgery as well as torn vaginal muscles requiring her to have a hysterectomy.

Police were called and Hunter would be arrested for rape, sodomy, kidnapping and domestic violence.

"And at that point, I feared for my life," Tracey recalled. "And I feared for my children's life."

A HIDDEN AGENDA

Hunter would be freed on bail but Tracey got a restraining order against him. She bought a gun and did not go anywhere unarmed.

She took photos of her injuries on the night of the alleged attack and texted them to Loran. Later, they would take more pictures.

Angered, Hunter would stop paying her spousal and child support. Tracey, however, may have had another scenario in mind for obtaining money.

She had forced Hunter to take out a $103,000 life insurance policy around the time their daughter was born.

On May 24, 2012, the day before Tracey shot Hunter, she would place a call to MetLife that was recorded.

"Thank you for calling MetLife, this is Pam. May I please have your name?"

"Tracey Grissom."

Tracey would then explain that she was angry that her husband stopped making payments on his policy. During their divorce proceedings, he had agreed to continue paying the premiums. Tracey stated she was calling to make sure that they had the correct address on file.

"Is there anything else I can do for you today?

"That's gonna be it!" Tracey said, hanging up.

"Well, May 14th was just like any other day," Tracey said, explaining the call to the insurance company. "However, I had moved four different times. Me and my children were running. We were running from Hunter. So I had called the company to let them know that they had my old address and to make an address change."

FALSE RAPE?

Shelly Standridge was hired by Hunter to defend him in the rape case. She would state that Hunter denied raping or even assaulting Tracey that night. Hunter did, however, admit to the fact that he and his wife had consensual sex that night...Rough consensual sex.

"So that night," Standridge said. "Hunter said that she was depressed and claiming she was going to kill herself. She was saying she wanted their relationship to work."

So she undressed in front of him. Her beauty was always impossible for Hunter to resist.

The two had sex despite Hunter having a new girlfriend at home.

Hunter's aunt, Gina, believed that Tracey wanted to kill Hunter before the rape case went to court.

"He had a new girlfriend, he was living with her," Phelps said. "He was moving on with his life. Hunter would claim that Tracey was jealous, obsessive, even stalked them."

"Hunter had moved on," Hunter's aunt said. "There was some court dates coming up that would prove that Hunter was innocent. There were court dates coming up that he would get visitation to his daughter. She had a lot to lose."

Tracey was on the anti-anxiety drug Klonopin. Hunter would tell his attorney that Tracey would take more than her prescribed dose. Because of this, she fell and cut her head. Hunter would then leave the house around 10:30 pm and go to his father's house. Tracey would call him hours later, at 3:20 am.

Hunter would state that Tracey had called to threaten him. She told him if he didn't want the responsibility of the children then she would make it where he would never be able to see them again.

Hunter's attorney did not know what Tracey's motive was for crying rape. She was very upset that he had a girlfriend.

MORE LIES...

Hunter would be arrested nearly twelve hours later, to his total shock.

Tracey would give her side of the story to the police which later is proven to be false.

She would tell police that Hunter had thrown her against the bathtub around 10 pm and claim to be unconscious until 4 am the next morning.

"But her phone records show she was on the phone all night, so she was never unconscious," Standridge said. "She was also using her data at 10:42 that night. She was using it again at 10:50 that night. ... She sends a text to her boyfriend at 1:49 am. She sends a text to her friend at 2:07 am. She sends another text to her boyfriend at 2:07 am."

Tracey would blame the calls on Hunter.

"All I do know is I was not the only person using my phone that night," Tracey said, suggesting that Hunter used her phone.

Medical records would show that Tracey's head wound was "purely superficial".

Only one suture was needed.

Furthermore, there was nothing on the medical record to support the fact that Tracey experienced vaginal and rectal tears. She did have bruises on her ankle and legs but the photos taken by police at the emergency room would not resemble the same photos that Tracey and her friend Loran would take days later. In the photos taken at the emergency room, an area of Tracey's body has no bruises. Days later, there is discoloration.

Tracey's attorney would blame the discrepancy on "blood thinners" which would cause Tracey to bruise easily.

There was also a discrepancy in her phone records. She would take a photo of her inner thigh, a deep bruise. This area of her body was not photographed by police during her emergency room visit. But on December 9th, almost two weeks later, Tracey took a photo of her inner thigh with the deep bruise

"He (Hunter) told me that he would make it to where nobody would ever want me," Tracey said after a 2010 attack. "I didn't report it because I thought he would kill me."

THE FINAL STRAW

Tracey woke up pissed on May 15th, 2012.

Hunter had been ordered to pay $2,100 a month for the rest of his life. He was not complying with the court order claiming that he was "out of work."

Tracey stated that she was on her way to a job interview when she saw a Grissom Construction sign out of the corner of her eye.

She stated that her initial plan was to take a photograph of Hunter at the job site in order to show proof that he was working as part of her litigation.

"I was getting ready to take the picture and when I looked up he was standing almost directly towards the front of the boat trailer," Tracey said. "He was looking back directly at me. He had this face, that's like mean - just, I don't know how to describe it. I mean, I see it over and over like it's right there all the time. He flipped me the bird, which to me was kinda like, 'Yeah I'm workin. Screw you.' And at that point, I panicked. At that point, I didn't know what else to do except to defend myself."

Tracey started firing. The first shot hit Hunter in the arm. He started to run and she fired again repeatedly. One of the bullets punctured Hunter's heart and he died of massive internal bleeding.

William Dockery was working with Hunter and was an eyewitness to the shooting. Hunter had turned to Dockery before the shooting and told him to "call the law". Before Dockery could pick up his cell phone, Tracey had commenced shooting.

Tracey then pulled out her own cell phone and called the cops on herself. She tearfully described that she had just murdered her husband.

CONFESSION

Tracey told detectives exactly what was going through her mind when she came upon Hunter at the construction site.

"Tell me about what happened," the detective said. "What led up to...what's going on."

"In November of 2010, he beat me unconscious and raped me...and, and left me for dead....and, and I finally pressed charges against him and he told me that he would make my life a living hell...and that's what he's done."

"What, what happened this morning that led up to you going..."

"I was going to work and I saw him...and he's been claiming that he-he's not working. And, so I pulled in there to take a picture of him...cause it was the truck that's still in my name...and the boat that's still in my name...and the trailer that's still in my name...He just stared at me and flipped me off...and I just went in there and shot him...I just shot him, I shot him, and I shot him."

Tracey would be distraught and tearful during her interrogation room confession. A few weeks later, however, she would call the insurance company to let them know that Hunter had died.

"Well, I was actually calling because I didn't know what I needed to do ... Hunter passed away May 15th and I actually am going a court case right now because it was due to self-defense..."

Hunter's family went ballistic over this. Tracey would claim that she had no money but she continued to pay his life insurance premiums.

"Even through the times when she's screamin' that she's destitute and has no money ... she continued to pay life insurance premium," Hunter's mother said.

"I don't think my sister concocted a story," Tracey's sister said. "Just so she could get insurance money. ... But that's all they (the prosecution) had."

THE TRIAL

Tracey's allegations of rape and sodomy would not be allowed in court testimony. She was allowed, however, to detail the effects of Hunter's abuse on her were.

Taking the stand, Tracey would lift up her shirt in court and show herself wearing a colostomy bag. She stated that she had undergone several surgeries after her husband's daily rapes wherein she suffered permanent rectal and vaginal damage.

Hunter's family was then allowed to speak at the hearing.

"This tremendous loss has changed me," Hunter's mother, Melanie Garner said. "And I don't know how to change back."

Chloe, Hunter's sister, had a victim's services officer read her letter in court.

"Tracey is psychotic," Chloe wrote. "She is the most selfish person human being on this earth."

"Every mother should pray every night that your son doesn't fall in love with someone like Tracey," Hunter's aunt, Gina Grissom said. "There have been lots of allegations against Hunter. We've never believed anything that has come out of her (Tracey's) mouth."

His aunt then looked directly at Tracey.

"Hunter was proud of his name. Why would you still choose to use our name, and bring it down?" suggesting that if Tracey hated him so much why didn't she go revert to her maiden name after the divorce.

The jurors would find Tracey guilty of murder. She would be sentenced to twenty-five years in prison.

One of the jurors, Janice Kelly, would contact Grissom's attorney Warren Freeman the morning after the trial. She had remorse over her decision and said that she wouldn't have convicted her had they had the rapes and abuse allegations been introduced as evidence.

"I feel I made a mistake," Kelly said. "If I had to do it over again, we'd have had a hung jury. We didn't get her side. She did not get a fair trial."

"We voted to convict because there was no dispute that Tracey shot Hunter," the jury foreman wrote in a letter that was addressed in the courthouse. "Jurors didn't believe prosecutor claims that she did it in order to collect a life insurance policy. We felt the shooting was a crime of passion, not for financial gain and that she should be sentenced accordingly. I wish we had seen evidence of the rape allegation. We feel that she just 'lost it.'"

"It's not fair, it's not fair!" Tracey sobbed as she was led out of the courthouse and to jail.

"We think the sentencing was too harsh," Tracey's attorney Warren Freeman said. "Considering you have the foreperson of the jury actually saying, we don't feel like she should be punished according to being found guilty of murder. Let's just say that there will be a basis for a new trial, and part of it will be something that the jurors saw that they weren't supposed to see and I'm going to just leave it at that until I file my motion."

"My son died running for his life," Hunter's mother said. "I don't know what was running through his mind but I hear him say 'momma.'"

"People who think that I murdered him in cold blood," Tracey said. "Either don't know the whole story or don't know everything that's happened.

Tracey was asked on CBS' 48 hours if she regretted pulling the trigger on that fateful day.

"No," she said flatly. "Because if I hadn't I would be dead. I truly believe that."

"She has a way of making everything she does look right," Hunter's aunt, Gina scoffed.

DON'T KILL ME, GRANDMA!

ERICA BYRAM

Dorothea Puente became infamous in the 1980s for being the "Death House Landlady". She ran a boarding home in Sacramento, California and proceeded to steal the Social Security checks of her elderly and mentally disabled tenants. Those tenants who proved to be too troublesome would be given increased dosages of sleeping pills until they died. She would chop up the bodies and bury them in her backyard.

EARLY LIFE

Dorothea Puente was born Dorothea Gray on January 9th, 1929 in Redlands, California. Both her mother, Trudy Mae, and her father Jesse James Gray, worked as cotton pickers in Central California. Her father would die of tuberculosis in 1937 while her mother would die the following year in a car accident.

Dorothea was delusional so some parts of her childhood have conflicting accounts. She states that she was the product of two alcoholic parents and that her mother was working as a prostitute before she died. She claimed her father was mentally unstable and often threatened to kill himself with a gun pointed to his head in front of the children (Dorothea would sometimes claim to be one of fourteen children.)

What is clear is that she was orphaned at the age of nine. Dorothea would then live in different orphanages, claiming to be sexually abused at one in particular. Eventually, her relatives from Fresno took her in. In her later years, she would discount the fourteen children claim and state that she was one of three children who were all born and raised in Mexico.

Dorothea would marry at the age of sixteen to a returning soldier named Fred McFaul. She would have two daughters a year later. Dorothea would give up both daughters, sending one to relatives in Sacramento and the other for adoption.

Dorothea would suffer a miscarriage in 1948 and McFaul would divorce her that same year. Angry at the failure of her marriage, she lied to everyone about the divorce and said that McFaul died of a heart attack shortly after their marriage ceremony.

She then turned to a life of crime. She would steal and forge checks. Dorothea would be caught in a forgery scam, serving six months of a one-year sentence. She would meet another man and become pregnant again. Dorothea would put the baby up for adoption as she hardly knew the man and could not afford the baby.

In 1952, she would marry a Swedish man named Axel Johansson.

CHOOSING A LIFE OF CRIME

Dorothea Puente would be married a total of four times with two documented divorces. She had another daughter which was put up for adoption at birth. The two would eventually meet, however, in 1986. Her daughter would describe her birth mother in unflattering terms, saying that she had "no real personality."

Dorothea would divorce Johansson in 1966 and marry Roberto Puente, a man that was almost twenty years her junior. The union would last only two years but Dorothea would keep his last name.

"Interesting that Dorothea would keep the last name of Puente," forensic psychologist Paula Orange said. "It became part of her con. She used the Spanish surname to con people into thinking that she was of Spanish descent. It helped her get some clients later on as she would use her surname as some kind of ethnic connection with them as in the case of the Costa Rican Bert Montalvo. She also cultivated a harmless old lady exterior in order to get people to put their guard down. She would tell people that she was seventy when in fact she was only fifty-nine. This con, this illusion would aid in her avoiding detection from social workers, parole agents and even the police."

Married life did not deter Dorothea's penchant for crime. Moving on from check forgery, she would run a brothel before being caught and arrested in 1960. Her sentence was relatively light, serving 90 days before being arrested for vagrancy and serving another three months.

Putting on a veneer that she was rehabilitated, Dorothea began working as a nurse's aide, providing care for physically disabled people and senior citizens in their private residences. This experience put a an idea in Dorothea's head.

She would manage boarding houses and cater to the elderly.

Dorothea finagled her way into becoming a manager for a three-story, 16-bedroom care home in Sacramento. She would marry for a fourth time, to a "raging drunk" named Pedro Montalvo. The union would only last a few months as Dorothea now took to trolling bars looking for older men who were receiving Social Security. She had the ability to put together tall tales, most often that she was a "famous actress" and told these men of her movie roles in films that didn't exist. In these movies, she always played the "evil woman." She also promoted herself as a "holistic doctor" and would listen intently to the maladies of her disabled mark before offering a suggestion on how they could improve their health. These stories would always lead to her convincing her mark to become one of her tenants after which she would steal their government check. She would talk a few into becoming her tenants the she would steal their government checks.

ARRESTS AND MORE ARRESTS

In 1982, Puente would be arrested for drugging and robbing people she would meet in bars. She would serve two and a half years in jail before she returned to her boarding house duties.

"Dorothea struck everyone as a harmless figure," Orange said. "So when she started the boarding house no one in their right mind would see her as a threat. They saw her as a sweet old lady. Her boarding house was spotless, inside and out. You could take a white glove, run your fingers across the furniture and not come up with a speck of dust."

Puente was a meticulous gardener and neighbors would describe her as being "very protective of her lawn."

"If somebody walked on her lawn," a neighbor said. "She'd cuss them in language that would make a sailor blush."

It would be this same year that the murders began. Dorothea had a friend named Ruth Monroe who began living with her but would die shortly after from a pharmaceutical drug overdose.

"She was sad," Puente told police when they came to investigate. "Very sad. Her husband was dying."

The police believed her and the death was ruled as a suicide.

"This is the occasion where Puente learned how to game the system," Orange said. "She learned that if there was no crime scene there was no crime. The police found Ruth Monroe dead and really had no choice but to declare it a suicide as there was no evidence that a murder had taken place. That was probably the farthest thing from the mind of the police. How could this sweet old lady be guilty of drugging up her best friend then smothering her with a pillow. She just didn't fit the profile."

Only a few weeks later, the police would return as a tenant named Malcom McKenzie would claim that Puente was drugging and taking money from him. Puente would be investigated and charged with theft. Sentenced to prison for five years, she began a pen-pal correspondence with a man named Everson Gillmouth, a 77-year-old retiree living in Oregon. Puente was then released after serving only three years of her sentence and found the smitten Gillmouth waiting for her.

They soon began making wedding plans, Gillmouth quickly opening a joint back account as they moved into an apartment in Sacramento together.

In November of 1985, Puente would hire a handyman named Ismael Florez to install some wood paneling in her apartment. She paid the handyman and threw in Gillmouth's 1980 Ford pickup as part of the payment.

"My boyfriend no longer needs it," Puente said. "I'm also wondering if you could build me a box. Say six feet by three feet by two feet. Just need to store some books and stuff."

Florez agreed and Puente would fill the box with her "stuff". She then hired Florez to help ship the nailed-shut box to a nearby storage depot. Puente accompanied Florez on the trip until they reached the Garden Highway in Sutter County. She then told Florez to dump the box into the Sacramento River.

"Its just junk," Dorothea said.

Months later, a fisherman would discover the box sitting on the bank of the river. Police would open the box to reveal a horrendously decomposed body of an elderly man.

Everson Gillmouth.

But it would be three years before police would be able to positively identify Gillmouth. Dorothea would continue to cash his social security checks. She would write his family on his behalf, stating that he was "sick" and could not contact them himself.

NEW BOARDING HOME, SAME RULES

Puente would rent a different boarding home from the Odorico family in what would later be infamously called the "F Street Boarding House."

Dorothea charmed the Odorico family, keeping the house spotless. They thought of her as family and referred to her as "tia" (Spanish for aunt). Despite being unlicensed and on parole, Dorothea was allowed to manage the place and supervise tenants.

But Dorothea's reputation grew in the community. She gave to charities and went out of her way to help certain people when it attended to her needs. She went to a charity ball and California Governor Jerry Brown stepped across the room to kiss her on the cheek.

The Governor then asked her to dance to the delight of onlookers.

In 1986, Puente would strike a deal with social worker Peggy Nickerson in an effort to provide a home for senior citizens on fixed incomes.

"She was the best the system had to offer," Nickerson said as she referred over nineteen elderly people to Puente in two years.

Dorothea would be a "Godsend" to social workers because she had no qualms about accepting troubled tenants, elderly and disabled people who could be abusive and addicted to drugs.

But Dorothea simply wanted their money. By having them as her boarders, she would collect their money first and pay them as she saw fit. Parole agents would come and talk to Dorothea. They would order Dorothea to stay away from her senior citizen clientele to no avail. Dorothea was never cited.

"The parole agents definitely dropped the ball," Orange said. "They are overwhelmed with work but it was almost as if they turned a blind eye. Here was a woman who had a criminal record of forging checks, running a brothel, and stealing Social Security checks from the elderly. Somehow, someway, she was allowed to run a boarding house. It boggles the mind really but shows you how each part of the social system had a piece of the puzzle but no one connected the dots."

Puente played good cop and bad cop to her tenants. There were some who said she was cheap and detailed instances where she withheld both their mail and their money. But there were others who said she could be kind and would praise her cooking.

Despite her philanthropic veneer, Dorothea had an autocratic personality. If one of her tenants showed up late for a meal, they would be denied food. She would send them away then make the other tenants "say Grace" before the meal.

She also did not drive and used a local tax driver to shuttle her around town.

"She had a lot of rules," Dorothea's driver Patty Rohrbach said. "Number one, be punctual. Number two, do what I tell you. And we'll get a long just great. She was generous almost to a fault. She'd tip very nicely and make sure there was enough time on the meter to make it worth my while."

Dorothea had a routine. She would go to the local hardware store to get gardening supplies, then get groceries. On Sundays, she would go to church then go to bars to solicit possible clientele.

"Dorothea would target the down and out," Orange said. "She would go to bars and offer a listening ear to someone who looked disabled or elderly. She knew how to game the system and would give the person tips on how to collect more on their Social Security or disability check. Then she would hand them her business card and invite them to stay with her as a boarder."

"She called them 'throwaway people'," Rohrbach recalled. "She said 'everyone has abandoned them and I've taken them in.' And I thought it was a charitable situation created for people who had nowhere else to go."

Rohrbach wasn't the only one taken in by Dorothea's facade. Social worker Nickerson brought a man named Bert Montoya to live in Dorothea's boarding home. She had taken special interest in Montoya as the 50-year-old Costa Rican needed a place to stay desperately. He was an alcoholic schizophrenic, a man who constantly "heard voices in his head" but someone who Nickerson perceived as a "sweet, kind man."

"Montoya had been living in a place called 'Detox'," Orange said. "A shack of a homeless shelter that had little more than vinyl mattresses on concrete."

Dorothea took to Montoya almost immediately, sensing he was a lost soul in a teddy bear's body. Montoya had a kind spirit, he once found over two hundred dollars at a homeless shelter and turned it in. He was troubled but not dangerous.

He was someone Dorothea could take advantage of.

Dorothea would take Montoya around the home and introduce him to the other residents. First there was John McCauley, a loud mouth drunk that did all of Dorothea's bidding. Second was Ben Fink, another alcoholic who despite being Jewish had a swastika tattoo on his arm. Lastly, there was John Sharpe, a compulsive gambler who suffered from short term memory loss.

"Dorothea took Bert Montoya under her wing," Orange said. "Moreso than the other tenants. He liked the fact that he could call her 'momma' and she called him her 'honey bear.' The social worker was surprised at how well he had adjusted to living under Puente's care. But Dorothea used him as a trophy. She used him to show everyone how compassionate and nurturing she could be."

The other tenants began getting jealous of Bert, in particular, John McCauley.

"The other tenants were paying upwards of $300 a month," Orange said. "They would get room and board plus two hot meals. Bert would get all that for free. All because Dorothea had taking a liking to the kind yet simple-minded man."

Dorothea went so far as to set up Bert with a running tab at the local bar. Bert would come in to the tavern, drink no more than three beers, then be on his way.

As much as Dorothea took to Bert as her showpiece, Ben Fink was a thorn in her side.

Fink would drunk himself into a stupor and had an uncanny ability to achieve alcohol levels that would be enough to kill an elephant, let alone a human being.

One night, the compulsive John Sharp was watching a horror movie in his room when he heard a large thump. The sound came from the upstairs bedroom that belonged to Ben Fink. Then he heard large bumps coming down the steps, as if someone were dragging a body. He thought it creepy at the time but didn't investigate.

Ben Fink would then disappear from the boarding house.

No one thought anything of it, however, as boarding house occupants were a transient group of people. Dorothea herself would kick people out after a few weeks and sometimes tenants themselves would leave on their own accord.

Dorothea never liked Ben Fink. Bert Montoya was until one night he did something to get into her doghouse.

Bert had went to the local tavern and this time he had gotten so drunk that he passed out inside the bar. Three of the other tenants had to carry him back to the boarding house.

"The group of men that brought him back described Bert as 'blowing bubbles' through his mouth," Orange said. "So that opens up the possibility that he had something else in his system aside from alcohol. We could easily surmise that Dorothea had begun to drug him up and the alcohol only exacerbated his symptoms. But something had spooked Bert. Something prompted him to drink more than his usual amount. He was trying to medicate himself and forget something he had seen at the boarding house."

Bert then ran away from the home, walking miles in order to return to 'Detox', the homeless shelter downtown.

"I don't want to go back," Bert cried out when the Detox manager allowed him back into the home. "I don't want to go back."

WHAT IS THAT SMELL?

Tenants in the boarding house began complaining about a rancid smell that was coming from the empty bedroom upstairs.

This would later be labeled as the "Death Room".

When the owners of the home, the Odoricos, came to do their monthly inspection they couldn't help but notice the odor themselves.

"It smelled rotten," Ricardo said. "It smelled rotten in there."

"I thought it was the tenants,"said Laura Arebalo, Ricardo's daughter. "because some tenants they would not bath on a daily basis."

Dorothea deflected the complaints as expected. She would blame the neighbors, saying they must be cooking something that's "not right." Then when that sounded lame she would blame a broken sewage line.

But late at night, Dorothea would shampoo the carpet in the room, awaking John Sharp.

When tenants and the owner asked about the room, Dorothea would simply say it was a room that was "cursed."

It was the same room where her friend Ruth Monroe had died only a few years earlier.

Neighbors complained to the city and the Department of Health was called in. They did an inspection of the house and made Dorothea sign a few documents.

But the smell remained.

And Bert Montoya returned.

After over two weeks on the streets and sleeping at "Detox" he arrived back at Dorothea's door steps.

Bert wanted to slip back into the house unnoticed but Dorothea saw him.

"When they cross me," Dorothea said. "They don't cross me a second time."

Then Bert disappeared.

"There was a reason why Bert didn't want to go back to the house to begin with," Orange said. "He openly told the people at the Detox that he didn't want to go back. I think he saw something there. Mostly likely he saw them disposing of a body. Chopping up a corpse. Something had freaked him out and Dorothea knew he would eventually say something."

"Bert had become a problem for Dorothea," Sacramento Police Detective Cabrera said. "He might even bring the police. She couldn't allow Bert to bring attention to her. She apparently felt that there was only one thing to do."

MORE SUSPICIONS

Neighbors began taking note of the strange doings of a man only known as "Chief."

Dorothea thought of Chief as the resident handyman of the boarding home. She had the man do odd jobs around place even though he was an alcoholic. Neighbors saw that Chief carted off dirt and junk away in a wheelbarrow after digging in the basement of the boarding home. He then tore down a garage in the backyard and put in fresh cement.

Then Chief disappeared.

And the owners weren't pleased that Dorothea had put in a concrete patio without any consent on their part.

"One time I went to the house," Ricardo Odorico said. "And I found a concrete patio."

"I used to have lots of roses," Veronica Odorico said. "I liked roses. Then I went and saw that everything was different. I said (to Dorothea) 'What happened? You took out the roses. She said 'I don't like roses.' I used to tell my husband he gave her too much freedom. He said it was to improve the house. I said I liked it better like I had it before."

By May of 1988, neighbors no longer complained of a smell coming from Dorothea's home. Now they were complaining of a stench coming from Puente's backyard. Dorothea dismissed their concerns, telling them that she was using "fish emulsion" to fertilize her soil.

"We couldn't stand it," one neighbor said. "There was a sick smell in the air, and there were lots of flies in the area."

In November, of that same year, social worker Nickerson would arrive at Puente's boarding house to do a welfare check on her tenant, Bert Montoya.

Montoya had been last seen in August and Dorothea would tell the police that the man had "gone home to Mexico."

"Dorothea gave this huge elaborate story," Orange said. "But the social worker knew that Montoya would not have picked up and left without notifying her. Smelling something fishy, she notified the police."

Police initially believed Dorothea's story but returned after Nickerson stated that another one of her clients went missing after being in Puente's care.

"Dorothea was accommodating when the police came to question her," Orange said. "They could not do anything without her permission. They couldn't search the premises or even come inside her house. But she was very polite and allowed one of the detectives to look around the home. He found some medicine vials that looked suspicious. They had names of different tenants on the vials but they were all in one drawer of Dorothea's. Then the asked if they could look around in the garden. To his amazement, Dorothea remained cooperative and said it was okay."

The police began digging up Dorothea's back yard. Initially, the dig did not go well. The police unearthed eggshells, food and other articles of garbage. They discovered some leather-like material, with the detective describing it as "very opaque, leathery."

One of the detectives dug further and came upon what he thought was a tree root. He pulled on the "root" and broke it away.

It turned out to be a human leg bone.

And the leather-like material turned out to be decomposed flesh.

The police then discovered the first of several corpses on November 11th, 1988. They found two more the next day.

"It wasn't uncommon for old Victorian homes to have human remains in the backyard," Orange said. "People have dug holes in their backyards and have found bones that date back to the early 1900s. There were occasions where folks didn't have enough money for a proper burial so they buried bodies in the backyard to save money. Initially, that is what the police took the bones for. A case of an old time burial."

But news quickly spread throughout the town and people lined up around the home to gawk. The crowd swelled so large that the police had to cordon off the street. Hot dog and t-shirt vendors began to show up to sell their wares. One of the t-shirts had an elderly grandmother holding up a shovel. The caption on the shirt read "I dig Sacramento."

Dorothea then inquired with Detective Cabrera that she was going to "go for a cup of coffee" at the hotel. Cabrera himself walked her to the hotel to ensure that no one harassed her on the way.

The detective returned to the site and within twenty minutes, he unearthed another body.

"Where's Dorothea?" his Lieutenant asked.

"Dorothea would pay a cab driver sixty dollars to take her to Stockton," Orange said. "From there, she took a bus to Los Angeles."

The police remained on the premises and continued to dig. Three days later, they would unearth seven bodies. They would identify Ben Fink by his swastika tattoo. Dorothy Miller, an elderly alcoholic would be identified as well as Betty Palmer.

"One of the more gruesome finds was that of Betty Palmer," Orange said. "She had her hands and feet chopped off as well as her head. Police searched far and wide for her different body parts to no avail. They dug and even checked under the crawlspace of the house. It is believed that Palmer was Dorothea's second victim and she was perfecting her technique, removing whatever evidence of identification she could."

THE AFTERMATH

The police continued to search the boarding house but found no other bodies. They still believed that other murders took place and Puente had used other means to dispose of her victims.

"We are getting a large number of calls from people with relatives who have stayed there," the Sacramento Police said in an official statement. "There are a lot more than seven names."

Twenty five tenants of Puente were missing and unaccounted for as the police did forensic work on the seven corpses.

Meanwhile, Dorothea Puente remained on the run.

The search began for Puente and by November 17th, she had been spotted in a Los Angeles bar. She had introduced herself to a patron as "Donna Johansson" and began questioning the man about his disability income. She offered to move in with him and fix him "Thanksgiving dinner" despite only meeting the man.

"She invited the man back to her hotel," Orange said. "He found her charming but declined. She got up and left and he's watching television in the bar. A news report comes on and he sees Dorothea is wanted for murder."

The bar patron called the LAPD and Dorothea was arrested at her hotel. Detective Cabrera and other officials from Sacramento Police arrived in Los Angeles to take her back.

"I'm sorry, Detective," Dorothea said while sipping on a cup of coffee.

"Dorothea, I knew if we dig we're going to find more," Cabrera said. "I know that. I know that."

"Well, I didn't put them there," Dorothea said. "I couldn't drag a body any place."

"I believe that. But I believe there's somebody else involved here."

Cabrera knew that there was a distinct possibility that Dorothea had an accomplice.

"Bert Montoya weighed about two-hundred and fifty pounds," Cabrera said. "How does a person that's five-foot-three, five-foot-four, one hundred and thirty-five pounds carry somebody like that."

Resident John McCauley was arrested and questioned by the police. He was later released for lack of evidence.

The police went on to believe that Dorothea had unknowing accomplices, employing her tenants to dig the holes. She would cut the body into pieces. For the pieces she needed help with, she would roll the body part up in carpet or plastic and have someone carry it out.

THE DEATH ROOM

In December of 1988, forensic police work had positively identified four more victims that were uncovered at the Puente boarding home. The victims were Bert Montoya, Vera Martin, Dorothy Miller and Leona Carpenter.

There was evidence to believe that Carpenter was buried alive.

"She (Leona) was put in the ground shallow," Cabrera said. "It appears that her legs, the victim kicked her legs up. And in doing so compacted the dirt around her legs forming a little bridge."

The mystery remained about the smell of the "Death Room". There were no remains found in the room.

Yet the smell never went away.

"One thing I'll never forget is when I pulled the carpet back," Cabrera continued. "When I pulled it back, the most grotesque odor came out and I knew that it was putrefying body fluids. The thing is there was other people living there. And it (burying the bodies) was based on opportunity. When was the best opportunity to put the people in the ground. So these bodies would have to lie there (in the room) until a period or a time when she could get them into the ground. I was in those graves. There was no odor. There as no smell. But in the 'Death Room', the carpet. The body fluid had a smell that would knock you over....This was nothing more than a house of horrors."

THE MOTIVATION

The sum total of Puente's scheming and killing netted her more than $5,000 per month. In turn, she would take the clothing of her victims and donate them to charities.

"We would get calls from local charities," Cabrera recalled. "And they said they were given bags of clothing from Dorothea. Well, what a great way to get rid of evidence."

Dorothea would be brought to trial and prosecutors would describe her as one of the most "cold, calculating" serial killers in American history. No one ever witnessed her kill anybody but Dorothea would later reveal that she would use drugs to overdose her victims. Forensics would discover traces of a prescription strength sleeping pill in all of the remains.

The social security checks would continue to arrive at the residence despite the tenant being deceased.

Dorothea used part of her ill-gotten gains to get a facelift.

On December of 1993, Dorothea would be convicted on three counts of murder of the nine bodies discovered.

"The tragedy in looking back at this story is that it could have been prevented," Orange said. "No one took the time to investigate Dorothea's background. Different agencies knew different information about her yet no one collaborated. The true victims are, of course, the deceased. They were referred to Dorothea as the 'throwaway people'. People that when she dumped into the ground, no one came looking. The tragedy is that Dorothea was right. But for the circumstances surrounding the disappearance of Bert Montoya, who knows how many more murders she would have committed?"

She was sentenced to life in Chowchilla State Prison and she died in 2011.

DEATH ROW GRANNY

Georgia Johnson

It never ends.

No way.

No way am I letting this man demean and degrade me another day.

He's just like my father.

A binge drinker. And the binges were happening more and more.

He's on the road to nowhere and taking me with him.

It never ends.

First my father. Now him.

Fuck it.

I threw the cigarette on the blanket. I knew it was flammable.

Then I watched the smoke rise and smiled.

In Lumberton, North Carolina, Thomas Burke fell victim to a house fire which was caused by a burning cigarette. Investigative authorities thought that he had fallen asleep while smoking, leaving thirty-eight-year-old Velma Burke as his widow.

They didn't know that the fire was set by Velma.

Velma knew how to play the part of the grieving widow. She cried and gave the authorities the requisite crocodile tears. No one would believe that the murder of Thomas Burke would set off a series of killings performed by the seemingly kind and harmless church-going woman with the soft voice.

But Velma was a killer...

EARLY LIFE

Velma Bullard grew up as the second of nine children in the rural part of Sampson County, North Carolina.

Times were tough for the Bullard family. They would live on a small farm with no electricity, running water or an outhouse.

"They had to go outdoors," forensic psychologist Paula Orange said. "The entire family had to endure the indignity of going into the woods or using pots to shit and piss."

The home was small and cramped for the nine children. Velma would be forced to sleep in the same bedroom with her parents until the age of five.

Her father was a loom repairman (fixing an apparatus that was used to weave clothing) and an abusive alcoholic. Velma had an older brother, Olive, who were subject to his nightly beatings. Lillie, her mother, was too meek to protect her children from her husband's violent outbursts.

"She had the type of father who would not need any provocation," Orange said. "He would take out the pettiest frustrations, like not being able to find something around the house, and take it out on the children. Velma would become resentful toward her mother who was too weak or indifferent to stop her father from beating on the kids. She accepted his discipline as 'the way it was.'"

Velma would find school as a welcome escape from her dreadful home life. She loved her teacher and was an excellent student during her early grade school years. When she would return home from school, she took solace in the fact that her father would always arrive home late as he worked long hours at the textile mill.

"Her father Murphy had that Protestant work ethic in him," Orange said. "He accepted the long hours and low pay, seeing a kind of nobility in that. Only problem was, he would binge drink. Not store bought alcohol but homemade moonshine. After a couple of shots, he would be 'lit' and inflict his wrath on everyone in the house."

By the age of eleven, Velma would be forced to take on various chores around the farm. She would clean up the house, washing and iron everyone's clothing (eleven people). Her father would chastise her for not mending or sewing his work clothes properly as well.

"Her father was a stern taskmaster," Orange said. "Hell, you can say 'slave driver.' He would have Velma come home early from school days when the laundry got too backed up. Velma hated this and felt embarrassed. Her family didn't have much and as she grew older her classmates began to see her for what she was, a poor girl that was an easy mark for teasing."

Velma would grow to be 5'3" but gain weight as she got older. She would be mocked about her obesity, her shoddy clothes the gap between her two front teeth. She would also be called "knot head" after she ran head first into a boy at school which left a permanent contusion on her forehead.

By the age of twelve, Velma seemed to have taken on all of her mother's duties. She would cook all of the family meals in addition to performing cleaning around the farm house. She would miss school for days at a time as her father forced her to complete chores around the home before she could continue her education.

"Academic achievement was not at the forefront of her father's mind," Orange said. "Her mother was of little use because of her depression and mental illness. Velma was the oldest girl so she took on the duties of mom at an age where she should have been playing with dolls."

ANGER, ABUSE, AND CHURCH

Despite her father's verbal abuse and alcohol-fueled beatings, the family kept up a face of religious interest. Velma would be sent to Bible school every year until the age of thirteen. During her last year of Bible school, her father marked the occasion by buying Velma a silk pink dress with ribbons. Velma recalled the day as one of the happiest of her life.

The happiness would be short-lived.

Velma would claim that her father raped her when she was thirteen years old. She revealed this only to her pastor in her later years before she stood trial. Velma did not even tell her mother whom she did not think would believe the molestation took place.

"Things that went on inside our home when I grew up," Velma said. "Were kept inside."

At the age of fifteen, Velma continued to excel in school. Despite her chubby physique, she becomes adept at basketball and is pegged to be the team's star player for the upcoming season. But her father did not allow her to play.

"Who is going to iron these damn clothes?" he snarled.

The family then moved to Robeson county and switched from the Presbyterian denomination to Baptist. It was here that Velma would meet Thomas Burke and the two made it clear that they wanted to date. Once again, Velma's father would intervene, telling Velma that she had to wait until her sixteenth birthday until she could date.

The two waited patiently for her birthday to arrive and the following year Thomas would propose to her while they went to the movies.

Knowing that her father would not approve, Velma and Thomas eloped, moving to Dillon, South Carolina. Neither Thomas or Velma had any money as they both quit high school to get married. Thomas then went to work at a local textile mill.

"At this point, I believe that Velma began to realize that her life would not be that much better with Thomas," Orange said. "He literally has the same job as her father."

Economics forced Velma and Thomas to move in with his parents. This arrangement would last for a year until Thomas got a better paying job at a soft drink company.

At the age of nineteen, Velma would give birth to her first son, Ronnie. The couple would then move back to Parkton, North Carolina where they would remain in the same home for eleven years. Two years later, the young couple would welcome a daughter named Kim.

A CYCLE OF RELIGION AND ABUSE

The Burkes would be fixtures at the local Baptist church with Velma taking the reigns to teach a Sunday school class. But the prayers and sermons would do little to offset the growing ennui in the Burke home. Two years after giving birth to Kim, Velma would get hit by a drunk driver while crossing the street. She would be hospitalized for an extended period, suffering both physically and mentally.

Thomas' job at the soft drink company would not be enough to provide for the family. Velma would be forced to leave her small children at home and work in a textile mill just like her father. The couple would have different work hours, with Velma working nights and Thomas working days as they would take turns watching the children.

Velma would fall victim to the hard work at the mill and the stress of raising two young children. She began bleeding and her doctor performed a hysterectomy.

Velma's mother would take pity on the couple and give them one acre of land near their old farm. Thomas would build a three-bedroom home for the family but Velma was already going down a slippery slope. Her personality changed after the hysterectomy, claiming that she always felt "nervous and afraid."

Things would get worse as Thomas suffered a head injury in a car accident. He then began to drink heavily and begin to beat Velma.

"It was deja vu," Orange said. "Velma had, in essence, married her father."

One night, the couple argued and Thomas punched Velma in an alcohol-fueled tantrum. The police are called to the home and Velma sent Thomas to the state hospital to get treatment for his drinking. Her husband remains there for three days but when he returns home, his behavior is worse than behavior. He's angry at Velma for sending him to the "drunk tank". His alcoholism worsens and he would go on to lose his job because of absenteeism.

"Velma is thirty-five years old at this time," Orange said. "But she's an old thirty-five with crow's feet under her eyes and a hangdog look. She's had a rough life, not necessarily by her own design, and it has taken its toll."

Velma leaves the textile mill but then finds two different jobs in order to support the family. During the day, she works as a sales clerk in a Belk department store. At night, she goes to work as a machine operator in a cotton mill.

Thomas, meanwhile, would continue to drink.

He rages on a daily basis, on one occasion he pinned son Ronnie up against the wall and threatened him with a knife. Velma would faint during the encounter and be transported to the hospital. She was diagnosed as having a nervous breakdown and lapsed into a serious depression. The medical staff gave her tranquilizers to calm down. Velma believed that it was during this stint in the hospital that she became addicted to the painkillers.

"The drugs were helping," Orange said. "When nothing else did. So she wanted more and more."

Velma's children acknowledged that their mother's mood swings were due to the drugs.

Over the next three years, Velma would go in and out of the hospital for drug overdoses. After each visit, her addiction only grew as did her prescription list.

"She fell through the cracks in her own family," Orange said. "And in the system itself. Her family had their own issues to deal with as Thomas would abuse everyone on a daily basis. Finally, Velma did something she could control. She killed her husband."

On April 21st, 1969, Velma would drop a cigarette on the floor of her home and waited until her husband inhaled enough smoke to die.

His death, however, would do nothing to solve Velma's problems.

Her addictions and anxiety would only get worse.

A HOSPITAL FREQUENT FLYER

Velma would have another nervous breakdown after killing Thomas and lapse into a guilt-ridden depression. But seven months later, a co-worker at the Belk department store would introduce her to fifty-four-year-old Jennings Barfield. Jennings had emphysema and diabetes but Velma would marry him anyway. Unlike her marriage with Thomas which started out well, Velma's marriage with the older Jennings would be troubled from the start. Her drug addiction would escalate and Jennings would express his own regret at marrying her.

"I don't know why I married her," Jennings said. "All she does is pop pills all day."

After less than three years of marriage, Velma decided to part ways with Jennings. She didn't file for divorce, however, she decided to poison him with arsenic. She would later claim that she only meant to "make him sick."

Jennings Barfield was already ill and doctors had no suspicion that Velma was behind the death. Arsenic was a slow burn poison that could kill without detection. The autopsy called for no arsenic test and Velma had gotten away with murder once again.

But Seven months later, Velma would overdose on her prescription meds and become hospitalized. Her family recognized the pattern but could not wean Velma off of the drinks. She would remain hospitalized for three weeks.

Her personality seemed to change after the hospital release. She returned to work at Belk department store but kept being combative and argumentative with customers. Her boss knew of her circumstances and tried to coax her to do better. He took her away from the public contact and into the back stock room where he had her put pricing on the clothing items.

Her boss soon realized that Velma's addiction had gotten out of control. Velma would not be able to function in the back room, leaving tasks uncompleted as she would have her prescription medications delivered to the store.

"It is a hopeless situation," the store manager told Velma's son Ronnie before he fired his mother.

BROKE AND DESTITUTE

With no income, Velma would lose the family home as she no longer paid the mortgage. She would be forced to move back in with her parents and face the two people she blamed everything for.

Her father had grown ill, however, and would die from lung cancer shortly after Velma moved back into the home. She would feel bad about her father's death and admit that she had a love/hate relationship with him.

"I had learned to love him as much as I had hated him," Velma said. "He was so good to my kids. I think he tried to do with my kids like he wished he had done to us. He could not stand to see me correct them. If I would pick them up and spank them, he would ask me, 'Isn't that enough?'"

But after her father's death Velma self-medicated once again. She overdosed and was hospitalized for two weeks. Her family didn't judge, they instead thought she was "cursed."

"Velma needed psychiatric help," Orange said. "So she began medicating herself with deleterious results. She would "doctor shop" for different physicians who would be manipulated into giving her the drugs she wanted. Her addiction eventually grows until she becomes desperate for money in order to fuel the drug habit."

A MURDERER AND A THIEF

Velma began stealing from those closest to her, starting with her mother. Her mother confronted Velma about a missing check and Velma went ballistic.

"She had violent mood swings," Orange said. "The medication had completely changed her personality as she needed the drugs above all else. The people around her were not familiar with how to handle a person who had this kind of mental illness. So this made for a very dangerous cocktail for her and anyone close to her."

Hitting a new low, Velma took out a $1,000 loan under her mother Lillie's name. She put up the family home as collateral and forged her mother's signature on the documents. Velma then blew through the money and a month later took out another loan, once again using her mother's house as collateral. The following month, she emptied the checking account on her now deceased husband, Jennings. Two months later, the loan company began sending Velma overdue notices as she had not been paying off the loan.

"In Velma's mind," Orange said. "She had no other choice but to kill off her own mother."

Velma went to the local pharmacy and looked for bottles that had the warning of "fatal if ingested." She put the poison into a drink for her mother and watched as she drank the fatal elixir.

Her mother then began vomiting and lost control of her bowels. Within a few hours, her mother could not so much as walk and an ambulance was called.

Velma came to visit her in the hospital to finish the job. Armed with a Thermos, she made a special concoction of chicken soup and arsenic.

"Drink it slow," Velma said as she tenderly lifted the cups to the lips of her ailing mother. "Slow."

Her mother would eventually die of "natural causes" as no one suspected Velma of committing murder. Instead, she received sympathy.

"So sorry for your loss," hospital staff said.

"The thing with arsenic is that it shuts down the whole system," Orange said. "So hospital staff just chalked up her mother's weakness to old age. Checking for arsenic poisoning would be the furthest thing from their mind."

Velma showed the necessary emotion and received sympathy from friends and family. She then moved in with her daughter Kim and son-in-law Dennis who lived in a trailer park. She could not evade the authorities for long though as the authorities caught wind of Velma's check forgeries.

Velma reacted as she always did. She would run away and medicate herself.

"Her drug addiction kept pushing her into a corner and she saw no way out," Orange said. "So, this time, she goes to her son Ronnie's house and overdoses again, trying to kill herself. She falls and breaks her collar bone which laid her out in the hospital another three weeks."

But the police find her situation unsympathetic.

"We're sorry, Velma," the deputy informed her at her hospital bed. "But once you have been cleared for release, we will arrest you."

Velma would not have that. She tried to overdose again but this go around the hospital staff pumped out her stomach.

She was sent to court the next day and sentenced to six months in jail for the forgery. She is released after four months for good behavior.

NO REHAB HERE

Her addiction still unchecked, Velma returned to live with Kim and her son-in-law. She rummaged through the belongings of her son-in-law and stole a check, forging his name so she can get more prescription meds. Her daughter Kim now has caught wind of her mother's addiction, pleading with her doctors to stop prescribing her.

"In some ways," Orange said. "The doctors were just as guilty as she was. But back in the day, there was no way to cross-reference this stuff like we do now. Once she had her fill with one doctor she would go to the next and the next."

Velma's addiction prevented her from taking a forty-hour a week job. So she looked for alternative forms of income.

She would find a job taking care of the elderly.

Montgomery and Dolly Edwards would be her first clients.

"She found herself some easy targets," Orange said. "There didn't seem to be any legislative body in place that prevents sociopaths from caretaking the elderly. So Velma doesn't slip through any cracks, she just befriends the elderly couple and begins taking care of them."

Montgomery was blind and unable to walk. He was 93-years old and his 83-year old wife was too feeble to take care of him. They paid $75 a week for Velma to become their live-in caretaker.

All was good, at least in the beginning. But Dolly had a sharp tongue and would criticize Velma daily. Velma would keep a nice exterior unless confronted, saw Dolly has yet another wheel in her cycle of verbal abuse.

"It seemed to be a never-ending loop for her," Orange said. "Being forced to deal with verbally abusive people. Velma had long since snapped and Dollie simply had no idea who she was dealing with."

Velma began to plot out Montgomery and Dollie's demise until she meets their nephew, Stuart Taylor.

Stuart was already married but was blown away when he met the caretaker of his Aunt Dollie.

Velma would play it cool, stealing what she could from the couple in terms of petty cash and household items that had value. They outlived their usefulness to her within a year as Montgomery died of "natural causes". One month later, Dolly also passed away.

And again, no one suspected the sweet and soft-spoken Velma to have had anything to do with their deaths.

MOVING ON

Velma saw being a caretaker as a perfect front for her. She could steal as much money as she could and when the old folks detected something amiss she would simply poison them. After killing the Edwards' couple, she set the word out at church that she as available to be a caregiver. The pastor would refer her to Margie Lee Pittman who was seeking for a caregiver for her elderly parents, John Henry and Record Lee.

"She comes here twice a week," the pastor reassured Pittman. "She's a nice, kindly woman. You can't go wrong."

Pittman's father, John Henry Lee, was eighty years old when he discovered that his new caregiver had forged a $50 check on his account. He then fell violently ill, suffering through a spastic spell of vomiting, diarrhea, and convulsions. The doctors would chalk up his quick death to gastroenteritis but in fact, he had been poisoned with arsenic.

Velma played the caregiver role until his end. She attended his funeral and cried with the family, sending an ornate wreath (with money stolen from the dead man) to the proceedings.

For whatever reason, Velma spared Lee's wife and moved back to Lumberton, North Carolina to live in a trailer park. She began working as an aide in a nursing home and received word from Stuart that he was now a widow. The two began dating and she moved part of her belongings into his home.

"Stuart is a nice guy," Orange said. "He has no idea what kind of woman Velma is. She is so manipulative and cunning that the younger man is putty in her hands. So the relationship starts great as she reels him in with kindness and charm."

The couple are happy cohabitating until Stuart Stuart finds a letter addressed to Velma from the state penitentiary.

Curious, he began reading the correspondence and realized that is from a former cellmate of Velma.

Stuart became enraged. He threatened to "expose" Velma to all of his family and friends. Somehow, someway, however, she was able to calm him down.

He then found out that she had forged over $200 in checks on his account. The two argued but stayed together for the next two months.

"Velma had the Christian facade down pat," Orange said. "She asked Stuart to forgive her and the next thing you know they are going to a Rex Humbard revival. But before they went, she poured arsenic poison in both his beer and tea. She made sure he drank every drop."

Returning home from the revival, Stuart started to vomit on the drive home, the poison kicking in.

Velma had to keep the con going. She had to appear like a concerned girlfriend so she called up Stuart's daughter, Alice, later that night and told her that Stuart had came down with the flu.

Stuart's daughter expressed concern but Velma kept her at bay.

"Don't you worry now, honey. I'll take care of everything."

Stuart died the next day.

Velma would speak at Stuart's funeral and tearfully asked for his wedding band. His family graciously allowed her to have it and gave her $400 to help her cope with the grief.

But Alice knew her father was a picture of health. She vociferously argued for more tests beyond the standard autopsy and sure enough, arsenic had been found in Stuart's tissues.

On March 10th, 1978, the sheriffs arrived at Velma's home to bring her in for questioning. She was interrogated for over three hours, holding her ground. But she knows the evidence will trump her denials and tries to commit suicide after being released. This go around, however, her son Ronnie stopped her.

The sheriffs come to visit Velma again and she has one more surprise up her sleeve.

But Velma has one more surprise up her sleeve.

She would confess. Not only for the murder of Stuart but of six others.

"I set my first husband on fire," Velma confessed without an attorney present. "And I killed the rest of them."

"It was almost as if she wanted to be free of the guilt she had been carrying," Orange said. "Her confession seemed to take a burden off her back."

"The last ten years were like that," Velma said. "A drug nightmare. It was a case of not knowing where you are or what you've done."

The bodies of her victims were later exhumed and all tested positive for arsenic.

FACING THE GRIM REAPER

Velma's case would be prosecuted by Joe Freeman Britt, who was listed in the Guinness Book of World Records as the country's "deadliest prosecutor."

Velma would plead not guilty by reason of insanity but the court denied her plea.

"I needed to keep them sick until I could pay back the money I had stolen from them," Velma said. "I wanted to earn their thanks by nursing them back to health. I needed the money. I was addicted to pain killers. Anti-depressants. Amphetamines."

On November 23rd, 1978, Velma's trial would begin in Elizabethtown, North Carolina where she would be charged with the first-degree murder of her boyfriend, Stuart Taylor. The trial lasted seven days and the jury reached a verdict of guilty, placing her on death row at the age of 47. She was scheduled to be executed on February 3rd, 1979 but received a stay.

Velma would be sentenced to death and the verdict was appealed all the way to the U.S. Supreme court. Her attorney maintained that the jury had never been presented with the full extent of Velma's "addiction and background." Velma remained tight-lipped about that to everyone but her pastor. Her attorney felt thought her horrific background could have been used as part of her defense and the jury would have found her to be more of a sympathetic case.

CHANGING SPOTS?

"She's not the same person who went to prison in 1978," Kim Burke Norton, Velma's daughter said.

While in jail, Velma became a model prisoner.

"The first week I was here was the worst week," Velma recalled. "Everything about it."

Velma no longer had access to her drugs in prison and she began to dry out. With daily visits from two different pastors, Velma began to discuss her anger and repressed issues that fueled her addiction and murders.

Velma would claim that as she was awaiting trial in 1978 she came to a "meeting with Christ" that caused her to "change inwardly."

Velma heard a broadcast by radio evangelist JK Kinkle. "Jesus loves you, prisoners, too," Kinkle said. "He died for you too. No matter what you've done, the Lord will forgive you."

After Velma heard this sermon, she dropped to her knees and cried out to God.

She would then become the "go to" counselor for young inmates in the prison.

The inmates would nickname Velma as "Mama Margie" because of her wisdom and she would in turn think of them as her "adopted children."

The prison guards and counselors would take the most incorrigible prisoners and place them in a cell next to Velma. Velma would invariably counsel the young prisoner and advise them on the correct path.

"They'd come in ready to kill themselves," Sister Mary Teresa Floyd said. "And here she was with a death sentence, mothering and helping them."

"Living in prison is a struggle," Velma said. "Even at its best. And I know that without Him and His strength that has sustained me, I couldn't have made it even this far."

Her stay on death row soon became a part of the news brief. During this time, a phalanx of evangelists would take her cause to the mainstream. The Reverend Hugh Hoyle would become Velma's personal minister as she received stays of execution in September, October and December of 1981. She would also have a letter correspondence with Ruth Graham, Billy Graham's wife as well as meeting their daughter Ann.

While Velma impressed the Christian do-gooders, the family members of the victims were not taken in by her "conversion."

"She's got religion now, they say," Margie Lee Pittman said. "Well, she had religion before. So we all thought."

A few more stays were granted until 1984 when the U.S. Supreme Court justice Warren Burger granted her a stay until August of that year. At this point, however, her execution seemed inevitable. In an ironic move, Velma would choose poison rather than the gas chamber and enjoyed the final visits from her children and grandchildren.

During the final week before her execution, the Reverend Hoyle, and his wife came to the prison with a battery-powered portable keyboard. His wife played the little organ then the Reverend sang "He Hideth My Soul" and "He is So precious to Me" in the cramped visitor booth.

Velma sang along, whistling in the graveyard before the reaper came for her.

She then wrote letters to each of the victim's family asking them for forgiveness. Reverend Hoyle would deliver the letters to the families, all of whom would refuse them.

MEET THE HANGMAN

As her execution date neared, Velma was placed in a solitary cell that stood directly across from the death chamber.

"It's total isolation," Velma said. "From everyone I had been with for six years."

North Carolina Governor James B.Hunt would reject her final plea for clemency.

On the day of her execution, the jail house would turn into a media frenzy. Death penalty advocates gathered outside the prison and chanted "Hip, hip, hurrah...K-I-L-L" while some sloganeered with "burn, bitch, burn". The protesters held up a few placards that quote Romans ch.13 which ironically was a verse that Velma would repeat to guards during her prison stay.

"For rulers are not a terror to good works, but to the evil...(The ruler) beareth no the sword in vain, for he is the minister of God, a revenger to execute wrath upon him that doeth evil."

The execution was scheduled to take place at 2:00 a.m but the protesters remained outside, their chants reduced to a simple "Kill her! Kill her!"

On November 2nd, 1984, Velma would be executed by lethal injection. The prison official came out and addressed the press, giving out copies of Barfield's statement of apology. The reporters then eagerly anticipated what Velma requested for her last meal. Initially, Velma just wanted the normally scheduled prison food; chicken livers, collard greens and a sheet cake with peanut butter icing. The last meal was delivered but Velma immediately lost her appetite. Instead, she opted for Cheese Doodles and a glass of Coca-Cola.

"Her attorney believed that Velma could have done some good in life," Orange said. "He stated that she could have become a teacher, counselor or a pastor. But her father set her on a path of self-destruction that she couldn't escape from. By the time she the left that road to ruin, she was too far gone in terms of her murderous acts. Justice had to be served in the end. In the end, the law doesn't care how genuine you are in your pleas for forgiveness. It only cares about the rule of law."

"I'm sorry for the hurt that I've caused," Velma said before her execution. "So many people, today if it were possible, I wish I could take every bit of hurt on myself."

KILLER SEDUCTRESS

GARY RACE

Shayna Hubers

Shayna Hubers is a 21-year-old graduate from Lexington, Kentucky. She grew up in a comfortably middle-class family and was a smart young woman. She graduated from Paul Laurence Dunbar High School in 2009, and went on to college. During high school, Shayna's friends described her as quiet and "most likely to succeed". Shayna graduated from Kentucky's prestigious School of the Arts after making Dean's list in 2012. She was in the process of pursuing a Master's Degree in counseling from Eastern Kentucky University when she took the life of her on-again off-again boyfriend, Ryan Poston and effectively put her life on hold.

Poston was a 29-year-old lawyer and business owner from a successful family of attorneys and executives. He was loved by his friends and family and admired by women. He was known to be friendly, respectful and respectable, and an overall good guy. He met Hubers in 2011 through mutual friends on Facebook and the attraction was instantaneous, as the first photos of Hubers that Poston saw were racy in nature. The two began to chat, and started officially dating shortly after they went on their first date. They continued their relationship for over a year. If it hadn't been for Facebook, the two more than likely never would have met, as Shayna lived 80 miles away from Ryan and had no reason to venture into Ryan's neck of the woods.

Throughout the entirety of the relationship, the couple sent thousands of text messages, including a conversation about possibly taking a two-week long break from each other and the relationship. Hubers was also known to post pictures of herself and Poston on Instagram. The seemingly happy couple exchanged over a thousand photo messages, as well as 20,000 messages through Facebook. Most of the Facebook messages had been sent by Hubers to Poston, who had responded to only a handful of them.

To people who weren't aware of the couple's dynamics, it appeared as if they were a happy couple who had everything going for them.

They were both beautiful, successful, and driven. It was a match made in heaven- or so it appeared to be, but the truth was much darker and would become the subject of a complicated trial and a life term in prison.

On October 11, 2012, Hubers and Poston and his family had dinner at the young lawyer's home. After dinner, Hubers went home- she returned a few hours later, however, and the couple got into a heated argument. Poston informed his girlfriend that he wanted to end their 18-month long relationship, and it set Hubers off into a fit of anger. Her anger worsened when she was later told that Poston already had a date lined up with the 2012 Miss Ohio, Audrey Bolte. It's believed that the news of Ryan's new date was what pushed Hubers over the edge.

In the morning, Hubers' mother drove two hours to pick up her daughter and the two went out shopping. They were out for most of the day before Shayna was dropped back off at Ryan's house, telling her mother that she wanted to stay with him. Despite her other asking her numerous times to come home with her, Hubers was adamant that she wanted to stay at Poston's house. Shortly after, Poston became aware that Shayna was planning to stay at his place- he used this time to inform her that he had another date and didn't intend to spend the night with her. By 9 o'clock that night, the young lawyer was dead on his dining room floor.

At 8:53 that chilly Friday night, Hubers placed a 911 call from Poston's condo and said to the responding dispatcher: "Ma'am, I have...I have...I have killed my boyfriend in self-defense".

The dispatcher then asked what happened, to which Hubers replied "He beat me and tried to carry me out of the house and I came back in to get my stuff. He was right in front of me and reached down to grab the gun. I grabbed it out of his hands and pulled the trigger".

The dispatcher then instructed Hubers to step outside with her hands in front of her. Hubers complied, and responding officer, David

Fornash's partner cuffed and took her away while Fornash himself went to investigate the crime scene.

Fornash and the other officers who responded to the scene, found Ryan Poston lying on his dining room floor next to a Sig Sauer .380-caliber pistol. The pistol, upon further inspection, was found to have belonged to Poston, who had a passion for guns. "...he would have them in his boot, he would have them in his holster..." says Poston's ex-girlfriend, Lauren Whorley, who claimed that Poston's love of guns made her feel safe.

Fornash went room to room, double checking that there were no other hiding in the apartment and upon finding Poston's body, officers found that he had been shot once in the back, twice in the head, and three times in his upper body. The coroner is called and Fornash sets off for the station where Hubers had been escorted into an interrogation room and sat waiting.

Meanwhile Poston, lying dead on his kitchen floor, was supposed to meet with Audrey Bolte at the Milford Inn bar for a night of drinks and harmless flirting. Poston, however, did not show up and Bolte went home feeling confused. When asked how she felt about him not showing up, Bolte said that it was odd for Poston not to show up or give some sort of notice that he wasn't coming, as he was a very responsible individual.

Friends of Poston claim that he and Hubers were never really in a committed relationship, as Poston lost interest in Hubers rather quickly and made several halfhearted attempts to break it off with her. In fact, by October of 2012, Ryan had made 3 attempts to sever Shayna's ties to him. According to text messages between Poston and his cousin, he was emotionally drained from dealing with Shayna. "I received 75 text messages from her. I am emotionally and mentally spent. I hope she leaves me alone" reads one message between the cousins. Despite this, Poston continued to go out with Hubers and pose for photos.

Shayna, confiding in a friend through text messages, said that Poston had told her that he's only with her because he felt bad when she cries. She is also quoted as saying: "My love has turned to hate."

In one particularly chilling message Shayna claims that "...tonight when I go to the shooting range with Ryan, I want to turn around, shoot, and kill him, and play like it's an accident." The next day, Shayna posts a photo of herself with a gun at the shooting range.

The night of the murder, Shayna was interviewed about the incident. Left alone in the interogation room, Shayne almost seemed proud of what she had done, reports Chief Bill Birkenhauer. He watched her on live camera snapping her fingers, dancing around, and muttering to herself "I killed him, I killed him."

Legally, officers were not allowed to interrogate her without an attorney present, so when she was brought into the interview room they didn't ask any questions. In fact, officers didn't say anything. Shayna, however, readily volunteered her story of how the events took place. She was rambling on for two hours before running out of things to say. According to officers, the men and women who took turns sitting with Shayna, quickly grew tired of her rambling and would have preferred to leave. "Shayna appeared to be nervous, or trying to cover something up" one officer said. "...her stories, after a while, stopped matching up and kept changing." This, according to the officer, might have been happening as a result of Shayna realizing that she was in over her head.

When speaking about Poston's death, Hubers said that she knew he was dead because he was twitching. Her exact words were: "Literally, that's when I knew that he was dead or close to it...the twitching...and that was it." She goes on to explain how she couldn't let him sit there and twitch. She couldn't stand to sit there and watch him die so she shot 5 more rounds into his body to finish him off.

In addition to building a case of self-defense and trying to convince officers that she deeply loved Ryan, she claims that "he was very vain...he wants to get a nose job...I shot him right here-" she pointed to her nose and continued her story "...and I gave him the nose job that he wanted."

Officers didn't buy Shayna's claims of self defense due to lack of evidence that Poston was ever abusive towards her. "She claimed that she was pushed and that he hit her, however, there were no visible marks or wounds at all on any part of Shayna's body" says former FBI profiler James Fitzgerald.

"There was no evidence in Ryan's condo that there was a fight" adds Laura Richards, a prominent criminal behavioral analyst.

Photos from the crime scene show evidence against Shayna's claims of a fight, as there were a number of pill bottles and bullets standing on end on the table. Had a fight taken place, they would have been knocked over or displaced and the murder area would have been left a mess. Instead, it was neat and tidy other than the pool of Ryan's blood that was left behind after the shooting. Shayna had also claimed that Poston had thrown her against a bookshelf. The bookshelf in question, when police arrived, was undisturbed.

As for Shayna's odd behavior when left alone, Richards believes that it was an act in an attempt to appear mentally unstable and open the door for the insanity plea should her self-defense claims fall short. "She couldn't decide which plea to go with- self-defense or insanity. So, she decided to open the doors to both and see which one panned out the best."

After three hours of deliberation, Shayna is charged with one count of first degree murder. In 2014, her trial is well underway and a forensic pathologist mentions that at the time he was shot, Poston had been sitting down- a fact that goes against what Shayna had said previously. According to Richards, this fact alone blows Shayna's claims of self-defense out the window as it shows that Ryan was not charging at her in a fit of rage, as she had previously claimed. Instead, he had been seated and had been seated great distance away from Shayna at the time of the murder. Forensic expert Howard Ryan backs this theory up by going into detail about the shots that Shayna fired at Poston. He says that the first shot was to Poston's head, a fact that is significant due to the lack of blood found on Ryan's shirt.

"If he had been standing up, the gravity would have brought it down...straight down the shirt through the bottom to the pants" he says.

Using the blood stains on the table, Ryan is able to provide further detail as to why he believes that Poston was sitting down. "When she shoots him in the forehead, his head goes down on the table." Poston's head would not have fallen onto the table if he had been in an upright position. From here, Ryan suspects that Poston's back was left exposed, setting him up for the next shot. At the same time that he is being shot a second time, his right arms falls limp and opens up the area of his body that will receive the third shot- which is right underneath of his arm. After this, his body slumps to the floor and remains there until it is removed by the coroner.

Three of Shayna's cellmates testified against her that day, claiming that she had told them that she intended to kill Ryan that night and that he had never been abusive to her. "She laughed about shooting him in the face and giving him the nose job he always wanted" claims Cecily Miller.

Another inmate, Holly Nivens, claims that Shayna made the whole abuse story up. When speaking about the bruises and scratches that Shayna would show people, Nivens claimed that Shayna inflicted them on herself.

Shayna also told her cellmates that she had messed the apartment up and thrown objects around to make it appear as though a vicious fight had taken place.

Shayna didn't take the stand, but prosecutors used her social media and interview footage as a substitution. Despite the overwhelming evidence against Hubers, her defense team maintained its argument that Poston had been abusive and that Shayna had acted out of self defense when she shot him.

A toxicologist was asked to plead in Shayna's defense and said that at the time of his death, Ryan had a strong mix of Xanax and Adderall in his system. He argues that these medications could have caused outbursts of anger and violence, making it possible for Ryan to snap and come after Hubers with a both his fists and then later on, a deadly weapon such as a gun.

A clinical psychologist was also called to testify on her behalf, and he diagnosed her with bipolar disorder with narcissistic tenancies, and post traumatic stress disorder (PTSD).

"She was very distraught. She was depressed" says the psychologist who claims that Shayna had told him that she had suffered from sexual abuse as a child, and was recognized as having alcohol and prescription drug abuse issues.

On the day of the trial, Shayna painted herself as a model girl friend to Poston, claiming that he had been going through a lot and that she had always been there for moral support.

"I was always good to him" she said.

Again, the jury didn't buy the story. Five hours after her trial started, Shayna was officially charged. She appeared back in court three months later for sentencing and was given 40 years behind bars. Shayna's defense team tried to lower the time before she becomes eligible for parole to 8 years instead of 20, but was denied this motion.

Just six months later, her legal team filed another motion seeking a new trial. According to her team, one of the jurors who convicted Shayna had not been legally eligible to convict her as he was a convicted felon himself. This, according to Kentucky law, made him unable to serve the court and gave Shayna's legal team a reason for a new trial.

It's said that Shayna's new trial date is set for early 2018. Until then, she is behind bars and serving her 40 year sentence as planned.

The new trial was originally set for January of 2018, but has been put on hold for 4 months longer at the request of Shayna's legal team. The extra time, according to her attorney, will be used to prepare.

Despite the 40 year sentence, Ryan's friends and loved ones are left with a sour taste in their mouths. Lauren Whorley, in an interview with a news station, claims that she wishes she would have known what was going on- maybe then she would have been able to help and prevent Ryan from getting too tangled up in Hubers. She also said that she believes the trial should have been handled in an "an eye for an eye" fashion, meaning that what Shayna did to Ryan, should have been done back to her as justice.

"Maybe it's traditional, old-school mentality, but if you kill someone, then you know, it's an eye for an eye. And what you due unto others should be done unto you" she said.

For her, however, the sentencing brought a sliver of much appreciated peace. "I was there when they read it" she said about the final verdict "It was the longest 30 seconds of my life."

Matt Herren, a close friend of Ryan, still struggles to make sense of what went wrong that night. "I think about him everyday," he says "You just don't think something like that will happen to someone you know."

Like Whorley, Matt wonders if there is something he could have done to prevent Ryan from suffering the fate he did. "I know a lot of people in his life feel the same way" he says to "48 Hours" correspondent Peter Van Sant.

Van Sant asked Herren what was lost when Ryan was killed and Herren responded with "He's the type of person you want in your life. Not just a friend, but a loving son, a protective, older brother. He had three younger sisters that he adored." Poston had cared deeply for his three younger sisters and only ever wanted the best for them. In return, they showered him with love and looked up to their older brother.

Ryan and his family had been close-knit, despite his mom and dad divorcing when he was a child. He was close to his father, and when his mother remarried, he grew an attachment to his new step-father, Peter Carter. Ryan thought of him as a second father.

According to Sarah Robinson, a woman who had grown up with Shayna, her future had seemed promising as well. Shayna had been a good student and was never in any trouble.

"I thought she was, close to genius, in my opinion" she said " I mean, she was always in AP classes. Always getting A's in everything."

During her academic career, Hubers had received various awards for academic excellence and leadership.

"She liked to succeed at anything and everything she did" Robinson concludes.

When Van Sant asked her what Shayna had been like with boys in high school, Robinson mentioned that Shayna could be dramatic. "If a guy, broke up with her or something, she would take it pretty hard" she explained "...crying, and a maybe a bit of screaming..she didn't really like to let things go."

When asked if Shayna had been happy with Ryan, Robinson said that as far as she knew, she had been. As far as she knew, they had both been happy.

Ryan's friend, Allie Wagner, claimed that there was something wrong with the relationship from the start when she was asked the same question about Ryan. According to Wagner, Shayna had been cold upon their first meeting. "You could just immediately tell that...that she was obsessed with him," she says.

"He was busy with work..he didn't really have time for anyone" Herren adds. "He didn't want to hurt her feelings..that wasn't the kind of person he was."

As Shayna's denial towards Ryan's disinterest progressed, he started to wonder if he might need to put a restraining order out against her. "This is getting to be restraining order level crazy..." he wrote in a text message to his cousin "She's shown up at my condo 3 times and refuses to leave each time."

Ryan's neighbor, Nikki Carnes claims that there may have been two sides to the tumultuous relationship. She says that Ryan may have been emotionally abusive. According to Carnes, Shayna complained frequently of Ryan putting her down. "She told me that he would say she needed a boob job or a face lift and that she was fat and needed to lose some weight" she says.

Van Sant then asked her why Shayna wouldn't have left and she replied "I guess because she was young and she always told me she loved him." Carnes also told Van Sant that Shayna did everything for Ryan from taking his dog outside to picking up and doing his laundry. On the night of the shooting, she also reportedly heard gunshots but didn't hear the couple fighting, as Shayna had claimed that they had.

Wagner, when asked what she thought could have happened that night replied, "I think she went over there...tried to talk him out of breaking up with her. And I think he just stood his ground for the first time," she said "I think he just said no, like, this isn't working. So she picked up the gun and shot him."

Chief Birkenhauer agreed with Wagner's theory "He wanted to break up with her...I think that Shayna was not gonna be broken up with" he said in an interview with Van Sant.

Prosecutor Michelle Snodgrass explains why Shayna's pleas of abuse were dismissed. "Someone who is in shock does not pirouette," she says in response to the police videos of Shayna singing and dancing in the interview room "Within hours of putting six bullets in Ryan Poston and watching him die, she was dancing and singing."

"There were hundreds of thousands of text messages. And most of them were from Shayna. For every 1 message Ryan sent, she sent probably 50," Snodgrass says "She couldn't stop herself."

According to Snodgrass, rejection was what ultimately pushed Shayna over the edge and drove her to kill the man she so desperately loved.

"Ryan's a bright guy; he's a lawyer" says Van Sant to Snodgrass "Why wouldn't he get a restraining order?"

"Under the law in Kentucky, he didn't qualify for a restraining order. The law in Kentucky required the two to have been living together or to have been married" she replied.

Van Sant then spoke to Hubers' mother, Sharon, about the tragedy. "She graduated cum laude in three years at the University of Kentucky. She was pursuing a Master's Degree in school guidance counseling," she said.

"And what do you want people to know after reading this" Van Sant asked "...in relation to this case?"

"Shayna Hubers is not a child, a girl, a person that would murder someone; that would wake up and say 'OK, I'm going to shoot somebody"

"I want the world to know who Shayna is. And I want them to hear it from her mother" she concludes tearfully.

Hubers and her mother had been close most of Shayna's life, according to Sarah Robinson. "I think she was very close to her mom. I think her mom, for a good portion of her life, could have been her best friend."

This statement is backed up by a quote from Sharon Hubers in her interview with Van Sant: "That child has been a blessing to me. She's my whole life."

"The word that has been used to describe your daughter is evil" Van Sant teold Sharon.

"She's far from evil. Shayna has a heart of gold. She's like her mommy...a loving spirit. That's what I want the world to know" she replied.

After the trial, Shayna spoke up for the first time. Despite having killed their beloved family member, she didn't apologize to Poston's family. Instead, she apologized to her family and friends, and speaks only of herself.

"I'm sorry to my family. And I'm sorry to my friends for letting them down. And I'm sorry for the money my parents had to spend on attorneys" she says, after being convicted of the murder.

"I do wanna help people. I do wanna be something better. And I do want to continue to grow and learn" she said to the judge "And I just don't think a 40 year sentence will help me. I don't think it would benefit me any."

Judge Fred Stine replied to Shayna's statement with his own choice words. "What I think happened in that apartment was little more than cold-blooded murder."

Regardless of what happened that night, a promising young lawyer lays dead, and a successful college student sits rotting behind bars. Two families have been destroyed, and law officials are left baffled. Both the victim and offender have been robbed of their lives- and for what? For a reason that the offender calls love.